Sculpting Her Body Perfect

Second Edition

Brad Schoenfeld, CSCS

**Personal Training Center for Women
Scarsdale, NY**

Human Kinetics

Library of Congress Cataloging-in-Publication Data

Schoenfeld, Brad, 1962-
    Sculpting her body perfect / Brad Schoenfeld.-- 2nd ed.
        p. cm.
    ISBN 0-7360-4469-8 (soft cover)
    1. Physical fitness for women.   2. Bodybuilding for women.   I. Title.
    GV482 .S37 2002
    646.7'5'082--dc21   2002005929

ISBN: 0-7360-4469-8

Acquisitions Editor: Martin Barnard
Managing Editor: Wendy McLaughlin
Assistant Editor: Kimberly Thoren
Copyeditor: Karen Bojda
Proofreader: Joanna Hatzopoulos Portman
Permission Manager: Toni Harte
Graphic Designer: Nancy Rasmus
Graphic Artist: Judy Henderson
Photo Manager: Carl Johnson
Cover Designer: Keith Blomberg
Photographer (interior): Terry Wild Studios, unless otherwise noted
Art Manager: Carl Johnson
Illustrator: Kristin Mount
Printer: United Graphics

Human Kinetics books are available at special discounts for bulk purchase. Special editions or book excerpts can also be created to specification. For details, contact the Special Sales Manager at Human Kinetics.

Printed in the United States of America   10   9   8   7

Human Kinetics
Web site: www.HumanKinetics.com

United States: Human Kinetics
P.O. Box 5076
Champaign, IL 61825-5076
800-747-4457
e-mail: humank@hkusa.com

Canada: Human Kinetics
475 Devonshire Road, Unit 100
Windsor, ON N8Y 2L5
800-465-7301 (in Canada only)
e-mail: orders@hkcanada.com

Europe: Human Kinetics
107 Bradford Road
Stanningley
Leeds LS28 6AT, United Kingdom
+44 (0)113 255 5665
e-mail: hk@hkeurope.com

Australia: Human Kinetics
57A Price Avenue
Lower Mitcham, South Australia 5062
08 8277 1555
e-mail: liaw@hkaustralia.com

New Zealand: Human Kinetics
Division of Sports Distributors NZ Ltd.
P.O. Box 300 226 Albany
North Shore City, Auckland
0064 9 448 1207
e-mail: blairc@hknewz.com

This book is dedicated to my brother, Glenn, who opened my eyes to the world of fitness. His guidance and encouragement inspired me to reach my personal best, and for that I am eternally grateful.

Contents

Preface

The odyssey began in 1997 when I decided to put pen to paper and detail my High-Energy Fitness™ system of training. I had spent many years developing and perfecting the system with my private clients and was eager to share it with the rest of the world. What better way to accomplish this task than in the form of a book? Soon thereafter, I teamed up with Human Kinetics Publishers, and *Sculpting Her Body Perfect* was born.

The response to *Sculpting Her Body Perfect* was nothing short of overwhelming: it received both critical and commercial acclaim, generated a huge amount of media exposure, was translated into several different languages, and ultimately became one of the top-selling fitness titles. My vision had come to fruition.

However, with the passage of time and valuable feedback from readers, I have been able to evaluate the best way to improve on the original work. I believe I have accomplished this task in this, the second edition of *Sculpting Her Body Perfect*. Here are some of the highlights that set it apart from the previous edition:

- **Revised warm-up.** The chapter on warming up has been completely redone. The warm-up itself has been streamlined and no longer includes a stretching component. This takes into account recent evidence showing that stretching before exercise provides little to no benefit in preventing injury. Given the importance of flexibility in overall fitness, stretching now has been given its own section with specific guidelines on the best way to remain limber and supple.

- **Modified routines.** In the advanced training chapters I have tweaked many of the routines based on my ongoing experimentation with different exercise combinations. To optimize muscular development, exercises must complement one another, working synergistically to create a whole that is greater than the sum of the individual parts. The new routines are meticulously designed to take advantage of this synergy; they're guaranteed to take your body to the next level!

- **Clarifications.** Numerous other changes have been made throughout the text to reflect current theory in biomechanics and exercise physiology. Exercise science is a rapidly changing field. New studies come out almost daily that alter or expand previous knowledge. I have kept abreast of the research and updated the text with the most relevant information wherever applicable.

- **New exercises.** Perhaps the biggest addition to the book is the dozens of new exercises that can be performed in the comfort of your own home. I received thousands of letters and e-mails from women who, for various reasons, could not work out in a health club. Now, everyone has the opportunity to enjoy the benefits of my program, even if they don't have access to fancy equipment.

All in all, I am confident you will be extremely pleased with this new edition. It significantly expands on the original version, providing a wealth of additional information for achieving your ultimate body. I look forward to hearing of your success.

Stay fit!
Brad

Acknowledgments

To Bob Silverstein for your diligence, patience, and sound advice in bringing this book to life. You're not only a great agent but also a true friend.

To Martin Barnard, Cynthia McEntire, and Wendy McLaughlin for trimming the fat and sculpting this book to perfection. Your insight and ideas are invaluable.

To my parents for supporting me in my dream. You've always been there for me.

To all my clients, past and present, at the Personal Training Center for Women, who helped me perfect the High-Energy Fitness system and provided the impetus for this book.

To all the trainers, past and present, who have worked at the Personal Training Center for Women and helped me impart the High-Energy Fitness system to a legion of women.

To Gina Guiliano, Amy Tutera, Clarissa Chueire, Anastasia Schepis, Linda Giulanti, Jackie Roberts, Michelle Gabriele, Cindy Goldmintz, and Jane Imburgia for making the photo shoot run so smoothly. Your professionalism is greatly appreciated.

To Joe Weider for helping me bring fitness into the mainstream and expanding my knowledge in the early years.

To Christina Young at Newmark Communications. You're the best publicist on the planet!

To Kiana Tom, Debbie Kruck, Laurie Donnelly, Carol Semple-Marzetta, Donna Richardson, Lovenia Tuley, Michelle Ralabate, Lori Ann Lloyd, Shannon Meteraud, Rikki Rife, Tina Jo Bagne, Karen Hulse, Michelle Bellini, and all the other great fitness models who have embraced the High-Energy Fitness system and lent support. Your endorsements mean a great deal to me.

To Allison Bookless, Amy Fadhli, DeeAnn Donovan, Nicole Rollolazo, Chisato Mishima, Tanja Baumann, Linda Cusmano, Brandy Flores, and Victoria Johnson.

A special thanks to Gold's Gym in White Plains, New York, for the use of their fine fitness facility in the photo shoot. You guys are the best!

Introduction

You are about to set out on a journey to physique heaven—a place where everyone has achieved peak physical condition. The long and winding road that leads to this paradise is not an easy one to travel. But with dedication, persistence, and patience—as well as a lot of sweat and hard work—you can complete the journey.

Make no mistake, exercise is a science. The human body is one of the most complex mechanisms in the world. No invention—be it computer, machine, or any other human-made device—can approach its intricacy. This makes designing a training program an involved process.

Women's fitness is particularly complex. There are many female-oriented challenges that affect the training process—issues that men just don't have to face. Although some gender differences are obvious, other more subtle variances also affect exercise capacity. Let's discuss the most relevant of these physiological and psychological obstacles in detail.

- **Women produce very little testosterone.** Testosterone is a hormone that is secreted by the testes (in males) and, to a lesser extent, the ovaries (in females). It has two main functions. First, testosterone is androgenic (i.e., masculinizing); it promotes male-oriented characteristics such as the growth of facial and body hair, male-pattern baldness, and deepening of the voice. Second, testosterone is anabolic (building); through a complex process, it interacts at the cellular level with muscle tissue to increase protein synthesis —the primary stimulus for initiating muscular development. Hence, there is a direct relationship between testosterone and muscle hypertrophy: the more testosterone you secrete, the greater your propensity to pack on muscle. The problem is that, on average, women produce only about one-tenth the amount of testosterone as their male counterparts. Clearly, this makes it difficult for a woman to significantly improve the quality of her muscle.

- **Women tend to readily store body fat.** Like it or not, women are the fatter sex; on average, they carry about double the amount of fat as their male counter-parts. This is largely due to the distribution of receptors in adipocytes (fat cells). Receptors can be likened to doorways; they either allow fat into or out of adipocytes. There are two basic types of fat receptors: alpha receptors and beta receptors. Taking the doorway analogy a step further, alpha receptors are the "entrances" that allow fat into adipocytes for long-term storage while beta receptors are the "exits" that let fat out of adipocytes to be burned for energy. It has been shown that specific adipocytes—especially the ones in a woman's lower body—have a higher percentage of alpha receptors to beta receptors (as high as 6 to 1, by some estimates) and therefore tend to hoard fat and hold onto it. Making matters worse, women get hit with a double whammy due to the effects of estrogen. Among its many functions, estrogen is integrally involved in the storage of body fat. Specifically, it exerts a regional influence over lipoprotein lipase—an enzyme that signals the body to store fat. In lower body adipocytes, estrogen stimulates lipoprotein lipase activity, causing fat to accumulate in this area. Conversely, estrogen has the opposite effect in the upper body, where it actually suppresses the activity of lipoprotein lipase and thereby impedes fat deposition. This site-specific response diverts fat away from the upper body and into the hips and thighs, producing the rounded features normally associated with a feminine physique.

- **Women are affected by hormonal fluctuations due to the menstrual cycle.** The menstrual cycle can have a profound effect on a woman's mood and sense of well-being. Many women develop cramps, nausea, and fatigue in conjunction with menstruation, sometimes accompanied by feelings of irritability and depression. Compounding matters, significant fluid retention and cravings for sweets are frequently associated with the premenstrual period, thereby inducing temporary weight gain and edema. These symptoms can be detrimental to a woman's psyche and hence make it difficult, if not impossible, to train with any degree of intensity during this time.

- **Women are subject to the body-altering effects of pregnancy.** When a woman goes through pregnancy, major biological changes take place within her body. Certain areas expand, others stretch, and still others sag due to the demands of childbearing. In particular, there is a dramatic increase in body fat levels. Fat is a primary energy source used for fetal development. It helps to nourish the fetus and fuel the growth and maturation of fetal organs, vessels and bones. In order to support these extra energy requirements, the body attempts to mobilize as much fat as possible. It does so by secreting a large amount of progesterone—a hormone that increases appetite. Progesterone levels remain elevated throughout pregnancy, bringing about the intense food cravings commonly associated with childbirth. In addition, there is a rapid proliferation of adipocytes. Thousands of new fat cells are created—most of them in the lower body region. What's more, thyroid function often becomes impaired, causing a dramatic slowdown in metabolism. All of these things can carry over into the postpartum period (including the effects from any surgery), altering a woman's ability to get into shape.

- **Women tend to be self-conscious about their bodies.** Most men are quite comfortable with their physiques. A guy can look in the mirror and believe that, by losing a few pounds, he's ready to compete for the Mr. America title. Women, on the other hand, tend to be much more insecure about their bodies. They generally see themselves as being fat and out of shape—regardless of their actual proportions. Some of the top fitness models won't go to the beach in a bathing suit if they are as much as pound over their competition weight. Not only is this mentality unhealthy from a psychological standpoint, but it also can cause neuroses that lead to eating disorders or overtraining (the detriments of which will be discussed later in this book).

- **Women are frequently intimidated by hard physical labor and strength-related activities.** In the not-too-distant-past, it was considered taboo for a woman to lift weights. Gyms were basically dark, dingy, basement-like clubs dominated by men. The vast majority of women perceived them as seedy, sweat-ridden dungeons that were primarily inhabited by brainless "muscleheads." Moreover, there was insufficient information and knowledge about the potential benefits of exercise for women; essentially, strength training was thought of only as a means to grow big and bulky, with little other utility. The prevailing belief was that it decreased femininity—in effect, "masculinizing" the female physique. Although this perception is slowly changing, there is still a prevailing reluctance on the part of many women to engage in intense physical labor—and you can't make significant improvements in your physique unless you're willing to train intensely.

Given all of these fitness obstacles, you might wonder whether it's actually possible to achieve your ideal physique. The answer to this is a resounding yes! By embracing my High-Energy Fitness system of training—a supercharged exercise regimen that simultaneously tones your muscles while reducing body fat—you will achieve your fitness goals. I have trained women in their 40s, 50s, 60s, and even 70s who have significantly improved their body's appearance. If you follow my system as described, so can you.

Bodysculpting is at the core of my system. Simply stated, bodysculpting is a method of strength training that creates a toned, shapely physique—as opposed to bodybuilding, which focuses more on building big, bulky muscles. Think of each muscle as a mound of clay. You are the sculptor—the bodysculptor—and can mold them any way you choose. You can add a little here, subtract a little there—do whatever you wish to create the look that you desire. Whether you want to build up, slim down, tighten, or tone, you are in control of your own physical destiny; if you put in the effort, results are all but assured.

I like to use the analogy that you should approach bodysculpting as if you were building a house. A builder constructing a house must first lay down a foundation. The foundation is what the house will rest on; without a solid foundation, the house will crumble. Next, the builder must erect a frame. The frame is built on the foundation and will support the floors and walls of the house. After the builder adds the walls and roof, the structure will begin to look complete. Finally, the builder can focus on adding the fine details of the house, such as marble tiles and mirrored walls, which give the house a finished look. The homeowner, at her discretion, can now make further improvements on an ongoing basis according to taste.

Similarly, in sculpting your body, you first must develop a foundation of muscle (body-conditioning phase). You need this foundation to have a base on which to work. This also increases the solidity of your connective tissue and the strength of your joints—necessary elements for training at intense levels. Next, you can begin the bodysculpting procedure by refining your muscles (toning and shaping phase). Your body will now start to take form, and your lines and curves will be accentuated with pleasing shape and symmetry. Last, you can fine-tune your physique by concentrating on details such as enhancing the shape of your biceps or firming up your inner thighs (targeted bodysculpting phase). This is where bodysculpting truly becomes an art!

In addition to shaping your muscles, training in a high-energy format brings about a phenomenon called excess postexercise oxygen consumption (EPOC). Simply stated, EPOC means that calories are burned at an accelerated rate following a workout session. This is over and above your resting metabolism. As a rule, the more vigorous the exercise, the greater the EPOC—and believe me, the High-Energy Fitness system is certainly vigorous!

EPOC is your body's way of restoring equilibrium. The primary mechanism here is oxygen. During exercise, a large amount of energy (e.g., ATP) is expended. To restore these energy supplies, oxygen consumption goes up exponentially. And because oxygen consumption is directly involved in causing fat to be utilized for fuel, EPOC brings about tangible increases in fat burning. In fact, caloric expenditure has been shown to increase by more than 13 percent after the completion of an intense exercise session, with metabolic effects seen for more than 16 hours, postworkout!

For best results, I highly recommend that you perform this program in a health club, preferably one that has a wide array of fitness equipment. Just as a builder uses a variety of tools to erect a house, you can benefit from using a diversity of fitness devices to sculpt your body. Although it may be possible for a builder to construct a house using only a hammer and saw, it obviously would be a burdensome task. The end product would be compromised, and the project would take a great deal more time than it would if the builder had available a full complement of power tools. Similarly, if your access to fitness equipment is restricted, the possibilities for your routine will be limited. Inevitably, this will delay or restrain your progress.

With that said, however, cost, convenience, and comfort are all valid reasons why some women prefer training at home. Accordingly, I have provided alternative home-based movements for many of the exercises that require a gym. If you should opt to go it at home, the following equipment will be needed:

- **Dumbbells.** Dumbbells are an essential component of any home gym. You'll probably need a set of 2-, 3-, 5-, 8-, 10-, 12-, 15-, and 20-pound dumbbells. Depending on your strength levels, additional dumbbells might be necessary.

- **Ankle weights.** Ankle weights provide increased resistance for bodyweight movements. Get ones that can accommodate 10-pound weight insertions. Depending on your strength levels, a second set may be necessary.

- **Elastic strength bands.** Strength bands simulate cable exercise movements. Because of their unique strength-curve, they are an excellent supplement to free weight exercises.

- **Bench.** For proper performance of many exercises, you need to have an adjustable weight bench. This allows you to alter the degree of incline, affording the ability to vary your movements and work your muscles from different angles.

Within each targeted bodysculpting chapter (6-14), I have included special workouts specifically designed for completing the program at home. Each workout gives you the exercises necessary for working the right muscles for the correct length of time complementary to the machine workouts. The exercise finder on pages xii-xiii serves as an easy-to-use guide for finding the home-based programs.

In summary, the High-Energy Fitness system provides you with all the resources necessary to enjoy success in the fitness arena. If you follow this system as outlined, you will achieve your goals—I guarantee it! Be aware, though, that the program I espouse is not a shortcut to physique heaven. On the contrary, it requires a great deal of hard work and disciplined effort to achieve desired results. With that in mind, you should be able to progress at a rapid, steady rate. In most cases, expect to notice visible changes in your body a month after undertaking the program. You'll feel tighter and firmer, and your clothes will begin to fit better. Soon, others will start to notice these changes, complimenting you on your appearance. Over the next several months, your fat will slowly melt away and, in its place will be lean, hard muscle tone. And before you know it, you'll have reaped the many rewards associated with fitness, including enhanced strength, improved posture, elevated energy levels, increased bone density, reduced stress, and, of course, a terrific body!

Exercise Finder

Sculpting the Ultimate Body

Before setting out on your training odyssey and beginning the High-Energy Fitness system described in this book, it is important to familiarize yourself with certain supporting concepts and techniques that facilitate its implementation. Let's review these issues in depth.

Set Goals

To get the most out of the High-Energy Fitness system, you should set short-term fitness goals that will motivate you to train. Most women have good intentions and are brimming with enthusiasm when they begin a fitness routine. Initially, they are eager to go to the gym and are committed to maintaining a regimented program of exercise. Within a short time, however, they begin to lose interest in working out. This usually is due to frustration, but personal issues, feelings of discomfort, impatience, and many other factors can cause enthusiasm to wane.

Goal setting is one of the best ways to maintain your motivation to exercise. If you have a clearly defined purpose to train, you are much more likely to endure, and even look forward to, your workouts. Of course, everyone has days when they simply don't feel like training. Sickness, family crises, and so forth can affect a person in the short term and decrease the motivation to exercise. If, however, you have well-defined goals that are important to you, you are likely to get back into your routine in short order.

Goals must be both quantifiable and attainable. Goals that do not meet both of these conditions are not specific and therefore not meaningful. It is difficult to achieve nonspecific goals, and failure is apt to result in frustration. Let's discuss the qualities of a specific goal in detail.

• **For a goal to be quantifiable, it must have measurable parameters.** For example, losing 20 pounds in three months is a quantifiable goal. You can weigh yourself today and again in three months to see whether you have met your goal. The scale will measure your weight loss. Other examples of quantifiable goals include reducing your waistline by two inches in a month or dropping one dress size in six weeks. Conversely, wanting to look good is not a quantifiable goal. This is subjective and not measurable by any defined standards. A "goal" like this is doomed to lead to disappointment and frustration.

- **For a goal to be attainable, it must be realistic.** For example, losing 20 pounds in three months is an attainable goal. Losing 90 pounds in three months is not. If a goal is not attainable, it can serve as a demotivator. An unattainable goal can make you feel that your training endeavors are pointless. It is better to set modest goals that are readily within reach. Attaining them produces a feeling of accomplishment and spurs you on to loftier goals.

Several techniques are useful in reinforcing your goals and sustaining your motivation to train. One such method is visualization. Visualize your entire body—your arms, legs, shoulders, and so on—and get an image of the way you want them to appear. Think of yourself in great shape, walking on the beach in a bikini, or wearing a sexy dress at a party. You might want to think of a woman whose physique you admire and envision yourself developing a comparable body. Let your imagination be your internal source of motivation, and, within reason, do not set any boundaries on what you can accomplish.

If you find it difficult to use your imagination as a motivator, find a picture of yourself when you were happy with the way you looked, and tape it to the refrigerator or put it on your dresser. It is common to feel that you are fighting an uphill battle and to lose perspective about your ability to succeed. By having a tangible image in full view, you'll reinforce the idea that you have the potential to look terrific. Every time you see this picture, it will remind you of your potential. And I can assure you that if you follow this program, you will soon surpass your previous best!

In short, think about what motivates you, and apply it to what you want to get out of your fitness program. You have to really yearn for something in order to maintain enthusiasm over time. Without a specific goal, you won't have a reason to put in the work necessary to achieve results. Give yourself an edge and make use of every possible motivator that is meaningful to you—it will inspire you to look great for life.

Once you accomplish a goal, you should immediately set new goals that reflect your mission to work out. This will keep your efforts focused and allow you to maintain a zest for training. You should also review your goals periodically to make sure that they are consistent with your present objectives. You'll often change your goals as you progress in your fitness endeavors. Reevaluating your position can help you stay the course.

Develop a Mind-to-Muscle Connection

Contrary to popular belief, weightlifting is more than just a physical endeavor. There is a large mental component associated with the activity, and harnessing your mental acuity can substantially improve results while decreasing the potential for injury. In fact, two people using identical workout routines will achieve vastly different results depending on the level of mental focus that they apply during training.

In essence, a mind-to-muscle connection is the ability to visualize a muscle and to feel it working through a complete range of motion during exercise performance. Rather than thinking about where you feel a muscular stimulus, it requires you to think about where you are *supposed* to feel the stimulus. This might seem like a foreign concept to many, and its relevance to training might not be initially apparent. However, until you are able to develop a mental connection with your

©Michael Galimberti

■ Weight machines help maximize your strength potential.

muscles, the effectiveness of your training efforts will be severely limited.

Many trainees believe that weight training is merely the action of lifting a weight from point A to point B. Unfortunately, while these individuals might perform an exercise with what appears to be satisfactory technique, they fail to adequately stimulate their target muscles. For example, in the lat pull-down (see pages 62–64), it is quite common for a trainee to feel the majority of stress in her biceps and forearms. Because the biceps and forearms initiate the movement of weight in this activity, the arms necessarily receive a good deal of stress during the lift. Hence, without applying the mind-to-muscle connection, the trainee can be inclined to use her arms, rather than the target muscles of the upper back, to lift the weight. Obviously, this diminishes the overall effectiveness of the exercise.

To maximally induce muscular stress, you must consciously visualize the target muscle and use that muscle exclusively to raise and lower the weight. You must be oblivious to your surroundings, with all outside distractions purged from your mind. As you perform each repetition, the target muscle must remain under continuous tension, and you must make sure it is the primary mover throughout the movement.

In the lat pull-down, for example, your entire focus should be on sculpting your back to muscular perfection. Accordingly, you must make an effort to pull the weight down with the muscles in your upper back without assistance from supporting muscles. When you reach the bottom phase of the movement, squeeze your shoulder blades together and feel a distinct contraction in your lats, mid traps, and rhomboids.

As you let the weight ascend, your back muscles should resist the pull of the weight. It is all too common for a trainee to concentrate only on the positive (concentric) portion of a movement and to mindlessly let the weight drop without control on the negative (eccentric) portion. Not only does this release tension from the muscle and compromise results, but also it substantially increases the risk of bodily injury. Maintaining muscular control throughout both phases of a movement results in optimal benefits.

As you return to the starting point of the lat pull-down, you should feel a complete stretch in the lats, and you should proceed without hesitation to the next repetition. Keeping your mental focus channeled in this manner directs the majority of stress to the muscles of your upper back and maximizes muscular stimulation to the region.

Know Your Muscles

From the onset of training, it's important to cultivate a working knowledge of muscular anatomy, especially the major muscles of your body. A common response to this statement is "Why do I need to know this? I don't care about the names or locations of my muscles. Just tell me what to do, and let's start working out." This short-sighted approach, however, will eventually set back long-term progress. Taking the time to learn the muscles of your body will help you immensely in shaping your physique and avoiding some common training mistakes. Following are the benefits of acquiring a knowledge of muscular anatomy:

- **It helps you visualize each muscle during training.** Your mind-to-muscle connection is enhanced when you are able to create a mental image of the muscles that you are working. Developing a mind-to-muscle connection allows you to isolate your muscles more effectively during training and to direct stress away from undesired secondary movers. Without a comprehension of muscular anatomy, you will find it difficult to develop a satisfactory mind-to-muscle connection and will subsequently fall short of your maximum potential.

- **It helps improve your exercise technique.** An awareness of muscular anatomy solidifies the form and function of various exercises in your mind. When you understand the physics behind weight training, you are better able to apply this knowledge to the biomechanics of exercise performance. Simply knowing the path that a weight must travel to target a specific muscle allows you to notice inconsistencies in your form.

- **It helps improve muscular control.** The ability to maintain control over your muscles helps you get more out of each repetition in a set. It's easier to exert more force in your contractions, thereby increasing muscular tension. Because muscular tension is one of the primary factors in bodysculpting, it follows that you improve your results by developing muscular control. This becomes even more important when you use advanced training techniques.

- **It helps improve your ability to assess your physique.** Knowledge of muscular anatomy allows you to be more in tune with your body. You'll begin to notice your muscles (and those of others) and understand how each muscle affects your overall proportions. This enables you to assess your physique and know which muscles are in need of improvement to achieve optimal symmetry.

While you now may realize that it is advantageous to acquire a comprehension of muscular anatomy, learning the various muscles admittedly can be a chore. The human body contains hundreds of muscles. Virtually every part of you—including your face, neck, torso, legs, and feet—has muscular components. Although learning about all of these muscles is an imposing proposition, at this point you need to develop only a basic awareness of your musculature.

Most relevant are the so-called show muscles of the body. These are the muscle groups that can alter the shape of your physique and help to produce aesthetic proportions. The fitness community generally recognizes nine major categories of show muscles. These categories encompass many individual muscles. For instance, the back is one of the major muscle groups. It contains several muscles, including the latissimus dorsi, rhomboids, teres major, trapezius, and erector spinae, among others. Individual muscles make up subcategories within the major muscle groups.

Table 1.1 shows the major muscle categories and their individual muscles. I have listed the muscles that are of the greatest consequence in bodysculpting—the ones that will have the greatest impact on your proportions. To keep it simple, I have neglected to mention many of the smaller muscles in the body. These smaller muscles tend to be secondary movers that act as stabilizers to the primary

TABLE 1.1   MAJOR MUSCLE GROUPS

MAJOR MUSCLE GROUP	INDIVIDUAL MUSCLES
Back	Teres major, latissimus dorsi, rhomboids, trapezius, erector spinae
Chest	Pectoralis major, pectoralis minor
Shoulders	Anterior deltoid, medial deltoid, posterior deltoid
Biceps	Biceps brachii, brachialis
Triceps	Triceps brachii
Quadriceps	Rectus femoris, vastus lateralis, vastus medialis
Hamstrings and glutes	Semitendinosus, semimembranosus, biceps femoris, gluteus maximus
Calves	Gastrocnemius, soleus
Abdominals	Rectus abdominis, obliques

muscles. They receive both direct and indirect stimuli during exercise performance that contribute to their development. Unless you are preparing for a physique competition, these muscles are of little consequence to your overall aesthetic proportions, and you won't need to target or isolate them.

A general understanding of the major muscle groups of your body is essential to understanding the theory behind the High-Energy Fitness system. Because your body contains only nine major muscle categories, this shouldn't be too difficult a task.

On the other hand, learning the individual muscles of the body is more involved. If you don't have a background in science, the names (which are derived from Latin and ancient Greek) are difficult to pronounce, much less commit to memory. Don't worry, however, about specific muscular terminology or about remembering each muscle. In bodysculpting, many of these names are shortened anyway; for example, the latissimi dorsi are called the lats, the rectus abdominis muscles are called the abs, and so on. You should simply understand which individual muscles belong to each major muscle group and become aware of their approximate positions in your body.

Figures 1.1 and 1.2 show the location of these muscles. You can use these diagrams as a reference when a specific muscle is discussed. At this point, develop a general awareness of these muscles and make an effort to visualize the shape they take once they are developed. For instance, the triceps brachii (shortened to the tri's in bodysculpting lingo) is a three-headed muscle on the back of the arm (an area where many women tend to get flabby as the years go on), opposite the biceps. When properly developed, the triceps resembles a horseshoe and gives the upper arm a tight, toned appearance. Visualizing the triceps in this fashion can reinforce your mind-to-muscle connection and help you to actualize your ideal physique.

Compound and Isolation Movements

To construct an effective training program, it's important to understand compound and isolation movements. These are the two basic types of exercises utilized in weight training. Both movements have distinct characteristics and provide unique options for shaping your physique.

As a rule, compound movements involve the action of two joints, while isolation movements involve only one joint. Consequently, many supporting muscles are involved in the completion of a compound movement. Certain

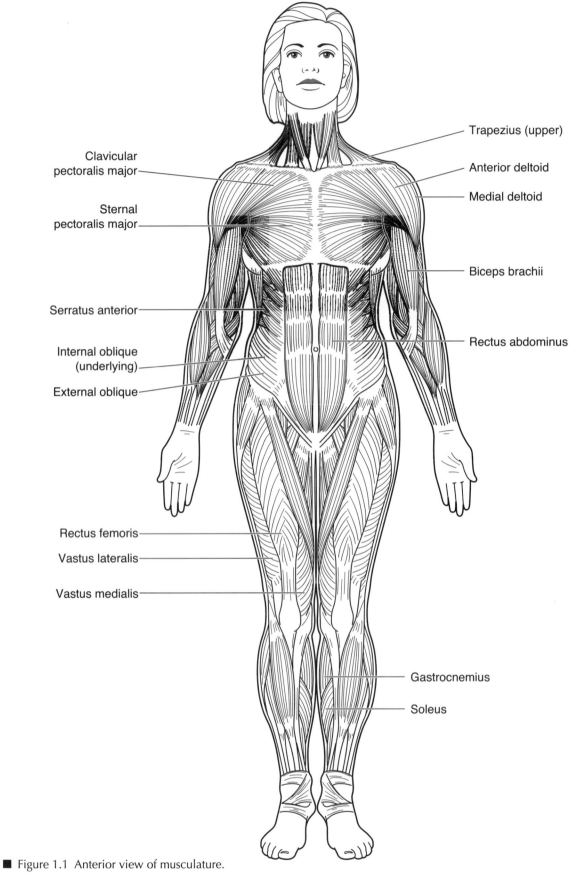

Trapezius (upper)

Anterior deltoid

Medial deltoid

Clavicular pectoralis major

Sternal pectoralis major

Biceps brachii

Serratus anterior

Rectus abdominus

Internal oblique (underlying)

External oblique

Rectus femoris

Vastus lateralis

Vastus medialis

Gastrocnemius

Soleus

■ Figure 1.1 Anterior view of musculature.

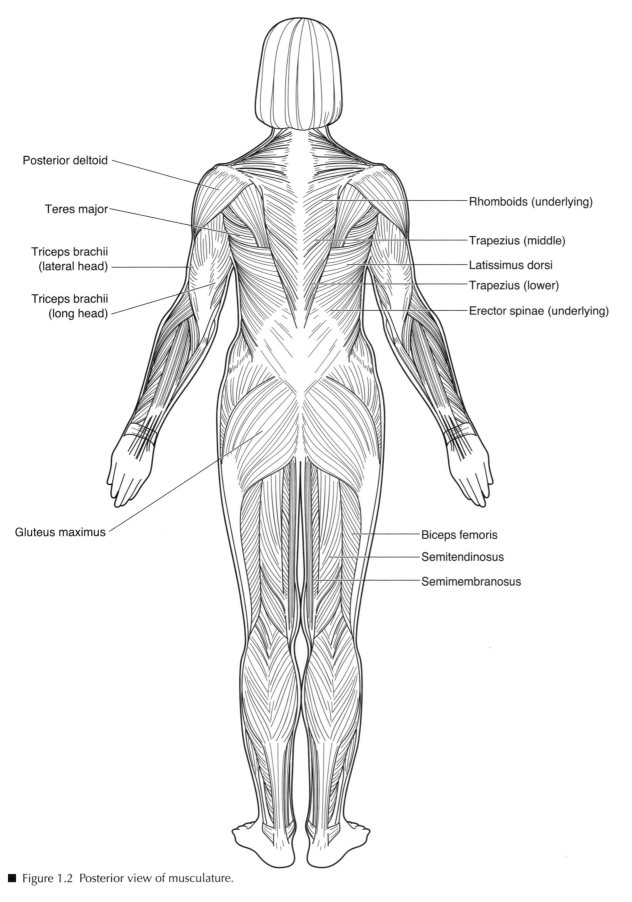

Posterior deltoid

Teres major

Triceps brachii
(lateral head)

Triceps brachii
(long head)

Gluteus maximus

Rhomboids (underlying)

Trapezius (middle)

Latissimus dorsi

Trapezius (lower)

Erector spinae (underlying)

Biceps femoris

Semitendinosus

Semimembranosus

■ Figure 1.2 Posterior view of musculature.

compound movements, such as the Olympic dead lift, require the use of virtually all of the major muscles of the body. In contrast, isolation movements tend to target a specific muscle or muscle group, excluding secondary muscles. Because only one joint is used to lift a weight, supporting muscles are less active during exercise performance.

For example, the squat (see page 137) is a compound movement because both the knee and hip joints are used to complete a repetition. As you descend into a squat position, both your knees and your hips bend to allow your body to move downward. Conversely, a leg extension (see page 143) is an isolation movement because only the knee joint is used. While both exercises stress the quadriceps primarily, they apply stimuli to different areas of the lower body. Most variations of the squat stimulate all the quadriceps muscles and provide secondary stress to the gluteal and hamstring muscles. In effect, your entire lower body is worked in this exercise (and, due to the stabilization required, even many muscles in the upper body). On the other hand, the leg extension stresses the quadriceps muscles, particularly the vastus muscles, almost exclusively. Virtually no stress is applied to the hamstrings and glutes. As you can see, understanding compound and isolation exercises is important to your training goals. The following paragraphs detail the advantages of each type of movement.

1. *Compound movements* are staple exercises in a fitness routine. They help to develop your proportions in a way that would be impossible solely by using isolation exercises. They are particularly important in the beginning stages of training, when overall development is of prime concern. Regardless of your training level, though, the inclusion of compound movements in your routine is an absolute necessity. These are some benefits of compound movements:

> • They strengthen the connective tissue supporting your muscles. If connective tissue is substantially weaker than its associated musculature, you are more prone to tendon and ligament injuries, such as pulls, tears, and tendinitis. The connective tissue works in conjunction with your muscles and must be strong for you to progress to the higher levels of training.

> • They help to stimulate many of the smaller muscles that are not specifically targeted by isolation exercises or single-joint movements. These smaller muscles assist in compound movements and thus help to shape the larger muscles. Moreover, they add detail to your physique, giving your body a polished appearance.

> • They provide an efficient means of training the body. Because you utilize many different muscles in the performance of a compound movement, you can do fewer total sets. This is especially beneficial when time constraints do not allow you to split your routine into exercises that target separate muscle groups.

2. *Isolation movements* allow you to isolate specific muscles. Isolation movements require the use of lighter weights than compound movements. Because supporting muscles are effectively taken out of the movement, the target muscle has to perform a majority of the work. These are some benefits of isolation movements:

> • They can selectively target a muscle at the exclusion of secondary muscles. The degree to which you can isolate a particular muscle is somewhat limited. It is influenced by where the muscle is situated in your body and by the range of motion of the movement itself. Nevertheless,

single-joint exercises are much more concentrated on an individual muscle. Thus, they tend to be better for developing muscular symmetry.

• They put less stress on the connective tissue than do compound movements. Because the amount of weight that you can utilize is substantially less than for compound movements, isolation exercises reduce the tension applied to the joints. This can be of particular benefit when you are training around a previous injury or medical limitation.

Table 1.2 lists some compound and isolation movements for the major muscle groups. Visualize each exercise and try to understand why it is considered a single- or multiple-joint movement. Once you are familiar with the difference, you'll be able to determine the type of almost any exercise and apply it properly in your routine.

Notice that the biceps and triceps are not included in the discussion of compound and isolation movements. These muscles, by nature, involve only one joint. The function of the biceps is to flex the elbow; the triceps extends it. All other joints must remain stable for proper stimulation. Consequently, any exercise for the biceps or triceps is an isolation movement.

Exercise Modalities

Another concept that you should understand is using several exercise modalities. To paraphrase an old saying, "Variety is the spice of exercise." To maximize your genetic potential, it is beneficial to employ a combination of machines, barbells, dumbbells, cables, and body-weight exercises. Each of these modalities has a unique combination of inherent benefits and drawbacks. By selectively combining them in your routine, you can heighten their advantages while minimizing their shortcomings. Following are the various modalities and their function in training:

• **Machines.** Exercise machines use air pressure, cams, chain connections, or other mechanisms. Machines generally offer a fixed path of movement, forcing you to maintain proper technique. This allows you to concentrate on the performance of a set rather than worry about your form. Moreover, a well-designed machine can provide less resistive force in weaker muscle positions and more force in stronger positions. Hypothetically, this allows you to maximize your strength capabilities, heightening your capacity to shape your physique. (Machines, however, do not adapt well to different body types, making this point open for debate.) Because controlling the resistance on a machine requires less skill, you reduce the chance of training-related injury.

TABLE 1.2 COMPOUND AND ISOLATION MOVEMENTS FOR THE MAJOR MUSCLE GROUPS

CATEGORY	COMPOUND MOVEMENT	ISOLATION MOVEMENT
Back	Lat pulldowns, rows, chin-ups	Pullovers, straight-arm pulldowns
Chest	Presses, push-ups, dips	Flyes, crossovers
Shoulders	Presses, upright rows	Raises
Quadriceps	Squats, lunges, presses	Extensions, kicks, adduction
Hamstrings and glutes	Good mornings, stiff-legged lifts	Leg curls, abduction

- **Dumbbells and barbells.** Also called free weights, barbells and dumbbells are excellent for developing muscular coordination and balance. They provide superb freedom of movement, so you can target individual muscles with better accuracy. What's more, free weights require that you stabilize the weight during exercise performance, activating your secondary muscles and thus helping to create a polished, symmetrical physique. As a rule, dumbbells are superior to barbells. Dumbbells force both sides of the body to work separately. You therefore can apply equal stimulus to each side. With barbells, the stronger side of your body can compensate for the weaker side. In addition, dumbbells are better able to move in line with the natural action of your body, thereby allowing greater range of motion. Accordingly, use dumbbells whenever possible, and use barbells for variety.

- **Cables.** Cables combine some of the benefits of free weights and machines. By providing resistance on both the positive and negative portions of a repetition, they supply continuous tension to your muscles. And because cables can move in three dimensions, they allow you to adapt an exercise to your individual body type (as opposed to a machine, which uses a fixed movement path). Cables, however, are not well suited for compound exercises, thus limiting their bodysculpting applicability.

- **Body-weight exercises.** A body-weight exercise uses your weight, rather than an external weight, for resistance. Body-weight exercises can be easy to perform (for example, the floor kick and lying abduction), somewhat strenuous (for instance, the walking lunge and push-up), or extremely difficult (for example, the chin-up and sissy squat). Although limited in scope, they can be especially beneficial when combined in supersets (which you will learn about later). In the short term, they provide a way to stay in shape when you do not have access to a gym. They are convenient and efficient, and you can perform them almost anywhere.

By combining these modalities, you have a wealth of exercises from which to choose. Consider the possibilities: you can perform many different variations of an exercise, such as the biceps curl, simply by varying the equipment you use to execute the movement. For instance, you could perform seated dumbbell curls, standing barbell curls, rope-cable curls, one-arm cable curls, machine curls, one-arm machine curls . . . the list goes on and on. Open your eyes to the potential for variety and you will improve your muscular development while preventing your workout from going stale.

Safety Precautions

You should take several basic safety precautions when using this program. You cannot improve your physique if an injury prevents you from training. Accordingly, observe the following important preventive measures.

- **Get medical clearance before undertaking this program.** Nearly everyone should get a yearly medical checkup to ascertain her state of health. If you are over 45 years old, a checkup is mandatory. Heart problems, hypertension, previous surgery, and other conditions can affect your ability to work out. The High-Energy Fitness system is an intense routine that requires a great deal of effort. A medical checkup allows a physician to identify restrictions or contraindications to exercise. If you have a medical condition, you may have to modify this program to accommodate your specific situation.

- **Take in fluids frequently while training.** It's a mistake to rely on thirst as an indicator of when to drink. Intense exercise inhibits the thirst sensors in your throat and gut; by the time you become thirsty, your body already is severely dehydrated. Therefore, during exercise, drink early and drink often. Consume eight ounces of fluid immediately before your workout, and then take small sips of water every 15 minutes or so while training, varying the volume based on your sweat rate. Sports drinks, although much hyped, do not provide additional benefit during exercise with a duration of less than a couple of hours. Moreover, they are usually calorically dense (using simple carbohydrates as their main source of calories), making them counterproductive to reducing body fat levels.

- **Wear a lifting belt and gloves during weight training.** Specially designed belts for weightlifting help protect your lower back from undue stress. The lower back is incidentally involved in many exercises and, because it is a vulnerable area, is prone to injury. A lifting belt helps to increase your intra-abdominal pressure, which provides additional support to the muscles of the lower back. Although it won't prevent a lower-back injury, it can alleviate stress to the lumbar region and thereby reduce the possibility of minor ailments. You should, however, remove the belt when you perform any abdominal exercises because wearing it reduces your ability to contract these muscles. It is also advisable to wear lifting gloves during weight training. These specially designed gloves help prevent calluses from forming on your hands, considered an unsightly blight by many women.

- **Learn to differentiate between soreness and pain.** "No pain, no gain" is a common battle cry in health clubs across the country, but this statement is misleading. Certainly, exercise must be intense and requires that you endure some momentary muscular discomfort. But you must know your body and be able to discriminate between muscular discomfort—a natural part of the training process—and pain related to an injury. If you feel sharp pain while working out, stop immediately and see a physician. If you are not sure of the source of the pain, it is better to cease training and wait a day or two before attempting to exercise again. Furthermore, if you feel dizzy during training, take some time to rest. If the dizziness persists, seek medical advice before continuing with your routine.

If you've had enough of the theory behind this system, you're in luck! You now know the basics you need to begin your journey to physique heaven. So put on your sweats, lace up your sneakers, and get ready to start your routine.

Warm-Up and Flexibility

Many women overlook the importance of warming up before their workout. The warm-up is not glamorous, nor does it appreciably affect the appearance of your body. Some women want aesthetic gratification and tend to shun activities that do not produce visible results. Consequently, they have a propensity to neglect the warm-up and begin training immediately upon entering the gym. When they are pressed for time, the warm-up is usually the first thing that gets blown off.

Make no mistake, however: the warm-up is an indispensable part of your workout, especially in the advanced stages of training. It prepares your body for the rigors of intense exercise by increasing range of motion, improving muscular responsiveness, speeding up recovery, and diminishing the possibility of serious injury. Those who choose to ignore this component jeopardize their well-being, putting their bodies at risk.

A warm-up can be divided into two distinct components: general and specific. In combination, these facets interact to thoroughly ready your body for vigorous activity. Regardless of your level of experience, the warm-up should remain simple and straightforward. Because the intent is to prepare yourself for intense training, not to challenge your resources, advanced techniques and fancy maneuvers are superfluous.

General Warm-Up

The general warm-up should always be performed first. Its purpose is to elevate core temperature and increase vascular circulation. There is a direct correlation between muscle temperature and exercise performance; when a muscle is warm, it can contract to a greater degree. As a rule, the higher a muscle's temperature (within a safe physiological range), the better its contractility. Simply stated, a muscle can produce more force when it is sufficiently warmed up, and this ultimately leads to better performance.

What's more, the warm-up increases the uptake of synovial fluid (via the synovial membrane), which enters the joint and provides the area with lubrication. And because body temperature is elevated, the viscosity of the fluid is reduced, causing a diminished resistance to flow. The net effect is an increase in range of motion and improved joint-related resiliency.

An excellent way to begin the general warm-up is with a period of light cardiovascular exercise. Virtually any cardiovascular activity can be used, including activity on a stationary bike, stair climber, or treadmill—the choice is up to you. Some people enjoy using a variety of different activities to reduce boredom, while others prefer to keep their warm-up constant. Either way is fine, as long as the basic objective is met.

Regardless of your chosen activity, you should perform it at a relatively low intensity, continuing only until you have broken a light sweat. A rule of thumb is to warm up at a level that is approximately 50 percent of your maximal heart rate (measured as 220 minus your age), adjusting your intensity as needed. Attempt to keep a steady, even tempo and concentrate on maintaining a stable pulse. Your resources should not be taxed, nor should you feel tired or out of breath either during or after performance. Your goal here is merely to warm your body tissues and accelerate blood flow—not to achieve cardiovascular benefits or reduce body fat. Consequently, if you are at all fatigued from your efforts, then you are warming up too hard. If so, reduce the pace of exercise and proceed in a more relaxed fashion.

Specific Warm-Up

During the advanced stages of training (i.e., targeted bodysculpting), it is beneficial to augment the general warm-up with a specific warm-up. The specific warm-up goes a step beyond the general warm-up. Not only does it help to further raise body temperature, but it also serves to enhance your neuromuscular efficiency in performing the particular activity. By using exercises that are similar to the actual activities in the workout, the neuromuscular system gets to "rehearse" the movement before it is performed at high intensity. Specificity is extremely important prior to intense training.

The exercises used in a specific warm-up should be as close to the actual training movement as possible. If, for instance, you are going to train your chest muscles, then some bench presses or push-ups are appropriate. A couple of light sets are all that are needed to achieve the desired benefits.

You're now ready to hit the weights!

Stretching for Flexibility

If additional flexibility is desired, targeted stretching movements can be added for even greater range of motion. If you incorporate regular stretching exercises, the sky's the limit as far as flexibility is concerned. By adhering to a regimented program of stretching, you can lift weights as well as maintain superior flexibility. You'll end up with a stronger body that is more resilient during physical activity.

When you stretch, go only to the point where you feel tension in the muscle—not to where you experience unbearable pain. If you stretch too far, your body sends a neural impulse to the overstretched muscle (called the stretch reflex), causing it to contract. This reflex actually tightens the muscle, creating an effect

RECUPERATION

Contrary to popular belief, training doesn't build up your muscles, it breaks them down. Intense exercise causes tiny microscopic tears to form in the working muscles. At rest, your body initiates healing to prepare for the next workout, when these muscles will be stressed again. Without rest, the muscles never have a chance to recuperate, and your body may become overtrained. Symptoms of overtraining include insomnia, fatigue, decreased motivation to exercise, flulike symptoms, depression, and increased frequency of injury. If overtraining occurs, you will no longer make gains in training and can even regress in your training efforts.

Because this program is intense, adequate recuperation is essential to repair muscle tissue and avoid overtraining. In most cases, the High-Energy Fitness system works best on a three-day-per-week schedule. Ideally, you should train on nonconsecutive days (i.e. Monday, Wednesday, Friday), allowing at least 48 hours for the muscles and central nervous system to recuperate from the previous workout.

Moreover, it is important to listen to your body and make adjustments in your routine based on how you feel. If you are run down, don't hesitate to take an extra day off. As long as you train consistently, an extra day or two of rest will not set back your efforts and can often help to rejuvenate your strength and enthusiasm. When in doubt, it is better to err on the side of caution and train a little less than to risk overtraining.

opposite to what you are trying to accomplish. By stretching slowly and taking your body to the edge without going over it, you can ease into a comfortable zone.

You should stretch your entire body, starting with the lower extremities and working up to the arms and torso. Stretch all your major muscle groups, regardless of the muscles that you have trained or intend to train that day. Give particular attention to areas that tend to be chronically tight, such as your hamstrings, hip flexors, and lower back. Although a single stretching movement is usually all that's necessary for each muscle group, unique circumstances, such as an injury or other factors, may require additional attention. When in doubt, spend a little extra time stretching, making sure that you are loose.

When to Stretch

It should be noted that the timing of when you stretch isn't as important as the fact that you do stretch at all. Stretching *before* exercise does little to prevent injuries. You can stretch all you want before training, but it won't diminish the chances of pulling a muscle or damaging connective tissue. This isn't to say that staying flexible is unimportant with respect to injury. On the contrary, it certainly is. There is a definite correlation between poor joint mobility and an increased incidence of exercise-related injuries, which is offset by flexibility training. Realize, though, that stretching does not necessarily have to be part of a warm-up in order to provide benefits; it can be done at any time, before, during, or after your workout.

In final analysis, if you choose to stretch before exercise, do so to improve flexibility—not to stave off injury. There is some evidence that stretching before exercise can cause a slight decrease in maximal strength during a training session, but this is of little concern unless you are involved in powerlifting or related activities. It even can be done on your rest days, as stretching won't have any negative effect on recovery. The important thing is to maintain good mobility in the joints, allowing them to execute full-range moves without restraint.

Remember, too, that excessive mobility leads to decreased stability. A joint that is hyperflexible is generally unstable. Thus, the goal of any flexibility program should be to achieve an optimal balance between mobility and stability within a functional range of movement.

Chest Stretch

From a standing position, grasp a stationary object, such as a pole or an exercise machine, with your right hand. Your arm should be straight and roughly parallel to the ground. Slowly turn away from the object, allowing your arm to go as far behind your body as comfortably possible. Hold this position for the desired time, and then repeat the process on your left side.

Biceps Stretch

From a standing position, extend your right arm forward with your palm facing up. Place your left palm underneath your right elbow. Slowly straighten your right arm as much as comfortably possible, pressing your elbow down into your left hand. Hold this position for the desired time, and then repeat the process on your left side.

Lat Stretch

From a standing position, grasp a stationary object, such as a pole or an exercise machine, with both hands. Bend your knees and sit back so that your arms are fully extended and supporting your weight. Shift your weight to the right to isolate the right portion of your lat. Hold this position for the desired time, and then shift your weight to the left.

Triceps Stretch

From a standing position, raise your right arm over your head. Bend your elbow so that your right hand is behind your head. With your left hand, grasp your right wrist and pull it back as far as comfortably possible, pointing your elbow to the ceiling. Hold this position for the desired time, and then repeat the process with your left arm.

Hamstring Stretch

Sit on the floor with your legs straight, and slowly bend forward. Allow your hands to travel down along the line of your body as far as comfortably possible. When you feel an intense stretch in your hamstrings, grab onto your legs and hold this position for the desired time.

Quadriceps Stretch

From a standing position, grasp a stationary object, such as a pole or an exercise machine, with your right hand. Bend your left knee and bring your left foot toward your butt. Grasp your left ankle with your left hand, and slowly lift your foot as high as comfortably possible. Repeat the process with your right leg.

Calf Stretch

Stand on a raised block of wood, an adjustable step, or another stable surface and grasp a stationary object for balance. Take your right foot off the block so that you are standing on your left leg. Slowly allow your left heel to travel downward as far as comfortably possible. Hold this position for the desired time, and then repeat the process with your right leg.

Shoulder Stretch

From a standing position, grasp your right wrist with your left hand. Without turning your body, slowly pull your right arm across your torso as far as comfortably possible. Hold this position for the desired time, and then repeat the process with your left arm.

3

Body Conditioning

The moment of truth has come! It is time to begin your journey to physique heaven, where you can redefine your body and realize your genetic potential. In earlier chapters, I concentrated on explaining the theory behind the High-Energy Fitness system—theory that is indispensable in your pursuit of a toned, feminine physique. I covered principles and strategies essential to various facets of fitness. The sooner you apply these concepts to the physical aspects of training, the quicker you'll reach your goals. If you understand the theoretical basis of the system, you can now put theory into practice. I recommend that you read over this chapter several times before beginning the program. By committing the routine to memory, you can focus your energy on training.

The body-conditioning routine is intended for those who have limited or no training experience. However, even if you have been training for a while, it's beneficial to begin with this routine until you are fully confident in your training abilities. When in doubt, it is better to start slowly and assess your ability as you move along. Skip to the next level only if you are prepared for a significant step-up in exercise intensity.

On average, a novice trainee should expect to remain on the body-conditioning routine for three to six months. This may vary, depending on individual factors such as initial fitness level, age, athletic ability, and so forth. As you gain training experience, try to assess your progress dispassionately. With the High-Energy Fitness system, you advance to higher levels of training in a stepwise fashion. By diligently following the system, you'll ensure steady improvement. Although there is a natural tendency to want to advance quickly, it's counterproductive to go to the next level before you are physically ready. Avoid the trap of seeking instant gratification. In the end, impatience will only serve to set back your training progress and sabotage your long-term goals.

The High-Energy Fitness system is intended to generate maximal results with minimal potential for injury. Compared with other activities, weight training is a relatively safe endeavor. Still, potential dangers are involved in working out. Studies show that novice trainees are at substantially increased risk of developing ailments related to training. The combination of inexperience and impatience at the beginner level can often lead to overexertion. Thus, the beginner must balance the aspiration to make appreciable gains with the need for safety.

You should realize that weight training can be awkward when you are starting out. Acquiring the various motor skills you need for exercise performance is a laborious process. This can have a negative psychological impact, often decreasing training desire. Be assured, though, that it is normal to feel uncoordinated and clumsy when first training with weights. After all, moving a resistant force through a fixed path, solely by using your muscular strength, is a lofty assignment. Fortunately, within a short time and with continued practice, these skills become second nature. Patience and persistence produce results.

To clarify the goal of the body-conditioning routine, let's revisit the analogy that compares bodysculpting to building a house. As a novice, your aim should be to lay a foundation of muscle on which to build. One of the biggest mistakes women make when they begin a fitness regimen is attempting to shape what they do not have. It is all-too-common for a woman to gravitate to the inner- and outer-thigh machines at the exclusion of all other exercises. Because you cannot spot-reduce body fat (see sidebar on page 21) specialized exercises have limited value until you develop a base of muscle. A builder cannot begin to construct walls or a roof before a foundation is in place. Similarly, you are the builder of your physique and must develop a foundation that will afford you the greatest potential for sculpting your body.

To build a foundation of muscle, this phase uses a total-body approach to training. You exercise each major muscle group every time you work out, providing broad-based coverage of your entire body. Total-body training allows you to work each muscle frequently, thereby stimulating the maximal number of muscle fibers in each training session. You repeatedly force your entire body to adapt to the stresses of training, helping to achieve overall development.

Initially, the thought of training your entire body every workout can be intimidating. Don't worry, though; it's not as hard as it may seem. As you will see, the system is configured in a way that optimizes your body's recuperative abilities and builds a foundation of muscle without completely draining your resources.

Body-Conditioning Protocol

In order to get the most out of the body-conditioning component of this system, adhere to the following protocol:

- **Exercises.** For each muscle group, you use only one exercise per training session. Each week you work your entire body three times. Although training your muscles this frequently can sometimes be overwhelming, the limited volume of the workload mitigates the risk of overtraining. By performing only one exercise per muscle group, you limit the amount of stress applied to each muscle. This allows you to quickly recover from a workout and to train each muscle on a regular basis.

- **Sets.** You should perform three sets of each exercise. This provides ample muscular stimulation without overtaxing your muscles. Do not move from one exercise to the next (as in a circuit routine). Rather, perform one set of an exercise, rest, perform your second set, rest, and then do your third set. This keeps the blood circulating through each muscle group, which increases your "pump" and thereby augments muscular development. After finishing three sets of an exercise, move on to the next muscle group and perform your subsequent sets in a similar manner.

SPOT REDUCTION

Perhaps the biggest myth in fitness is that you can "spot reduce" fat through targeted exercise. Make no mistake: spot reduction is a myth–a physiologic impossibility. Despite the inflated claims made by certain unscrupulous hucksters, individual exercises can't slim down a specific area of your body no matter how often or intensely you perform the movement. All the sit-ups in the world won't give you a flat stomach; no amount of lower body exercises will directly diminish the size of your thighs. In reality, trying to eradicate your problem areas with targeted movements is literally an exercise in futility.

- **Rest.** You should rest no more than 30 seconds between sets. This increases the aerobic benefit of the workout and therefore helps to expedite fat loss. In most cases, your routine will take slightly longer in the initial stages of training. As a novice, you are probably unfamiliar with the intricacies of training and preoccupied with matters such as your form, breathing patterns, and so forth. These factors tend to slow down your training pace. Still, it's best to keep your rest intervals as close to the suggested time limits as possible. Rest longer only if you are feeling dizzy or overworked. Your body will quickly adjust to a fast-paced tempo, and you'll soon be able to move from one set to the next without incident.

- **Repetitions.** The target is 15 to 20 reps per set. It is essential to train with good form and to apply continuous tension to your muscles during each repetition. Make an effort to develop your mind-to-muscle link early, making each rep count. From the outset, avoid the habit of trying to determine where you are feeling muscular stress. This passive attitude indicates that you are not properly visualizing the target muscle. Rather, think about where you are supposed to feel a movement. Your task is to mentally isolate a muscle or group of muscles, purging all other thoughts from your mind. Don't be concerned with your surroundings; whatever might be going on around you at that moment is irrelevant. Forget your troubles, your business dealings, your family obligations, and anything else not related to training. Concentrate only on performing each repetition with total focus on your target muscles.

- **Intensity.** You should perform all sets with a weight that is somewhat challenging without completely taxing your resources. In other words, by your final repetition, the weight should begin to feel a little heavy without causing you to struggle or compromise form to complete the set. As you gain strength, increase the weight to maintain the prescribed training intensity; remember, if the weight is too light to provide an adequate stimulus, you won't derive proper results. It is not advisable, though, to push the envelope at this point. Your body is not yet geared for intense exercise, and by training too hard, you'll invariably become overtrained.

Conditioning Protocol

Number of exercises:	1 per muscle group
Number of sets:	3 per exercise
Rest between sets:	No more than 30 seconds
Repetitions per set:	15–20
Intensity:	Somewhat challenging

The conditioning protocol summarizes the specific protocol of the body-conditioning phase of this system. Follow this protocol rigidly, with little modification. As you become familiar with the training process and progress to the more advanced phases of this system, you will have some flexibility to alter the structure of the routine. At this level, however, it is best to keep things simple.

Acclimating Your Body

If you have never trained before or have not trained for some time, consider your first few workouts an acclimation period. The goal should be to adapt your body to the routine and allow it to adjust to the stresses of weight training. Although you're probably already eager to see results, you should approach this phase as if you were about to swim in a cold pool. Obviously, it would be ill advised to dive headfirst into the pool without first testing the water; your body could go into shock from the extreme difference between body temperature and the temperature of the water. Similarly, your muscles, connective tissue, and nervous system experience shock from the demands of training, making it easy to overtax your body during this fragile period. If you are not careful, you can experience severe soreness, headaches, or injuries from overzealous efforts. These ailments can impede your ability to work out, thereby limiting results. Nothing can derail your exercise regimen more than an injury, so use discretion.

Moreover, conditions related to age can further inhibit initial training efforts. After the age of 35, a woman loses roughly 1 percent of her muscle mass and bone density each year. A sedentary woman will lose about 10 percent of her fundamental body mass by age 45, 20 percent by 55, and so on. Because this progression compromises strength and endurance, your capacity to train at an intense level is hampered at first. Consequently, the older you are, the more careful you should be to acclimate your body during the beginning stages of training. Although you can reverse the effects of aging, it will take a little more time, and an extra dose of patience is required. Training can have profound effects on improving bone density, strength, and other aging-related factors provided it is done properly.

Even with proper acclimation, however, you should expect to experience a mild degree of muscular soreness. This is especially prevalent in the first few weeks of training, but you may continue to feel sore even after becoming an accomplished trainee. Although the pain shouldn't be too severe, there will be some tenderness and sensitivity in the muscles that you trained. Unfortunately, soreness is a necessary by-product of initial training. It arises from microscopic tears that occur from the stress of weight training, which subsequently cause internal swelling in your muscles and connective tissue. Usually, the soreness lasts several days and slowly subsides as your body initiates the healing process. This is an indication that your body is adapting to the demands of exercise and preparing itself for the next training session.

It is important that you don't let muscular soreness inhibit or deter your training efforts. Working out during periods of mild soreness can help assuage it. Training aids the circulation of blood through your muscles and connective tissue, which can accelerate recuperation. If you are extremely uncomfortable and simply cannot train, take a few days off and use soothing remedies such as whirlpool baths or massage to alleviate the soreness. Try to avoid being completely sedentary, though; even mild activity can increase circulation to body tissue and accelerate the healing process. Of course, if you experience any sharp pain, stop training immediately and seek the advice of a physician.

Creating a Body-Conditioning Routine

During the initial four to six weeks of training, you should employ compound movements whenever possible. As previously discussed, compound movements stimulate the greatest amount of muscle, as well as strengthen your connective tissue and orient your nervous system to the demands of weight training. This will help you achieve balanced development from the outset and minimize the possibility of developing muscular deficiencies as you progress in your endeavors. The many variations of compound exercises permit you to add variety to your training and still meet this directive.

It's important to note the order of the exercises and how they relate to each muscle group. In the beginning stages of training, it's best to train large muscle groups first in your routine. Although it doesn't really matter whether you train your upper or lower body first, you should train the muscles of the torso (chest, back, and shoulders) before the arms (biceps and triceps) and the muscles of the quadriceps before the hamstrings. If you train smaller muscles first, they'll be less able to serve as secondary movers in exercises for the larger muscle groups. Ultimately, your secondary muscles will fatigue before your primary muscles, and you won't achieve maximal stimulation of the target muscle. For instance, performing a barbell curl will exhaust your biceps. If you then perform a seated row, your biceps will tend to give out before you fully stimulate the muscles of your back, thereby decreasing the effectiveness of the exercise.

Further, when training the upper body, it is best to alternate between pushing and pulling movements. The chest, shoulders, and triceps are used to push a weight, while the back and biceps are pulling mechanisms. Alternating these movements allows the antagonist muscle to rest for several minutes, thereby regenerating your muscular energy resources for exercise performance. Notice in the sample routine that you first train the chest (which uses the shoulders and triceps as secondary muscle movers), next the back (which uses the biceps), then the shoulders (which use the triceps), and finally the biceps and triceps in the upper body. In this way, you maximize muscular recovery between each exercise.

Using a training diary can help you move smoothly through your routine. A good strategy is to write down in advance the exercises that you will perform. You can then go through your workout routine knowing exactly what you are supposed to accomplish in the session. In this way, you won't aimlessly wander around thinking about which exercises to perform. The diary should include the exercises you used in each session, the amount of weight that you used in each set, and any notes that might help you in the future.

Table 3.1 details a three-day sample routine that you might use in the first four to six weeks of your training. These routines, like all the sample routines in this book, are only a guide to the possibilities for a diversified workout. A multitude of combinations are available for you to explore. Varying your routine will optimize results and help prevent boredom.

After the initial four- to six-week period, you should begin to incorporate isolation movements into your routine. Experiment with different exercises, paying close attention to the unique qualities of each movement. Make sure, though, that you do not neglect to include compound movements in your workout. These staple exercises, because of their all-encompassing effect, have great utility for beginners and advanced trainees alike. Mixing a variety of compound and isolation movements into your workout is a precursor to the next level of training, in which you will employ a split routine.

Table 3.2 shows a three-day sample routine that expands on the initial routine by combining a variety of compound and isolation movements. You should now be comfortable with the structure of this routine and should work on perfecting what you have learned. Again, get creative, and don't be afraid to try new exercises.

Doing so not only provides stress to a maximum number of muscle fibers but also helps to hone your performance skills for future gain.

TABLE 3.1   CONDITIONING PROGRAM: THREE-DAY SAMPLE ROUTINE

MUSCLE GROUP	DAY 1	DAY 2	DAY 3
Chest	Incline dumbbell press	Machine chest press	Push-up
Back	Front lat pull-down	Seated row	One-arm dumbbell row
Shoulders	Military press	Arnold press	Upright row
Biceps	Seated dumbbell curl	Cable curl	EZ curl
Triceps	Nosebreaker	Triceps press-down	Close-grip bench press
Quadriceps	Leg press	Squat	Lunge
Hamstrings and glutes	Good morning	Stiff-legged dead lift	Hyperextension
Calves	Seated calf raise	Donkey calf raise	Standing calf raise
Abdominals	Crunch	Jackknife	Reverse crunch

TABLE 3.2   THREE-DAY ROUTINE WITH COMPOUND AND ISOLATION MOVEMENTS

MUSCLE GROUP	DAY 1	DAY 2	DAY 3
Chest	Pec deck flye	Flat dumbbell press	Flat bench flye
Back	Reverse lat pull-down	One-arm seated row	Straight-arm pull-down
Shoulders	Shoulder press	Lateral raise	Bent lateral raise
Biceps	Preacher curl	Incline curl	Concentration curl
Triceps	Triceps kickback	Triceps dip	Overhead rope extension
Quadriceps	Leg extension	Sissy squat	Front squat
Hamstrings and glutes	Lying leg curl	Abductor pull	Seated leg curl
Calves	Seated calf raise	Toe press	Donkey calf raise
Abdominals	Rope crunch	Hanging leg raise	Twisting crunch

Optimizing Results in the Body-Conditioning Phase

When you execute unilateral movements (in which you train one arm or leg at a time), it is best to avoid resting between sets. In the one-arm dumbbell row, for instance, you should start with one arm, perform the target number of repetitions, go to the other arm, perform the target number of repetitions, and repeat this process without rest. Thus, one side is able to recuperate while you are working the other. By the time that you have completed one side, your alternate side should be fully recovered and ready to continue with the set. Because your body is never totally at rest, your heart rate remains elevated for an extended period of time, increasing the amount of calories expended.

As you try different exercises, you will probably find some movements uncomfortable or awkward to perform. This may be caused by several factors, including your body build, limb length, and others. Sometimes, even after repeated attempts, an exercise will just not feel right to you. If this is the case, simply drop it from your routine and move on to a complementary movement; there is no reason to keep the exercise in your training arsenal. You may decide, however, to try the exercise again after you have further developed your strength and motor skills. Often, you'll find that you now enjoy the movement and can realize additional benefits from the added variety.

You might wonder what to do if you are not able to perform a complete set of 15 to 20 repetitions of a particular exercise. In most cases, you should be able to decrease the weight enough to accommodate your strength level. But you'll probably come upon a few exercises that, no matter how hard you try, will defeat your effort to finish an entire set. This may especially be true in abdominal exercises and other movements in which your own body weight affects your strength capabilities. In these cases, simply perform as many repetitions as you can until your body gives out. Fortunately, strength and endurance tend to build up quickly, and you will see rapid improvement over time. With continued effort, you should be able to achieve your target repetition number for virtually any exercise.

When to Advance to the Next Level

After you have used the body-conditioning routine for a while, you will probably reach a point when you feel that you are ready to advance to a higher level. Understand, though, that taking the next step involves a significant increase in discipline and intensity. Each subsequent level of training requires a greater amount of effort. You therefore must use discretion in going forward. The question is, "How do I know when I am ready to take the next step?" In truth, there is no definitive answer. Before you continue, however, you should consider these points:

1. Make sure that you are knowledgeable about the basic principles of exercise. The mental aspects of training become increasingly important as you climb the ladder in your fitness endeavors. Understanding these principles will be crucial in maximizing results at the next level of training. Make sure that you clearly understand each principle and how it applies to the training process.

2. Make sure that you are comfortable with a variety of compound and isolation exercises. You should be able to perform dozens of exercises and be able to move readily from one to the next. Moreover, you should have a good grasp of exercise form and function and know the muscles that each exercise targets. In the next level of training, this knowledge will allow you to combine these movements synergistically with one another.

3. Make sure that you are willing and able to increase your exercise intensity. It's one thing to want to train on a more advanced basis; it's quite another to endure the intensity required for this progression. Many women do not realize the increased effort required to train at the next level. The body-conditioning routine is preparation for developing overall intensity of effort. You should gauge your ability to progress based on the difficulty you have with this routine.

If you are still not proficient or capable in all of these areas, take more time to develop your skills and mental acuity. Work on the basics, preparing your mind and body for more intense training. Do not pressure yourself to advance to the next phase. In fact, if you are happy with the way that you look at this point, you can continue with the body-conditioning phase indefinitely. Many women do not aspire to, or are not willing to train at, a higher level and are perfectly content with maintaining the status quo. This phase of training, however, will not allow you to actualize your genetic potential. Therefore, if you want to take the next step and begin the process of bodysculpting, advance to chapter 4 and read on.

Amy Fadhli

My story: I was 17 years old when I was in my first semester away at college. My twin brother was visiting me and told me I was starting to get cellulite on the back of my thighs! Imagine being only 17 and hearing that from someone who's not supposed to judge you! Well, it worked. The next week I joined a gym…

Achievements: 1996 Miss Fitness America

©John Abeyta/www.AFADHLI.com

What do you consider your best fitness accomplishment?

Finishing a mini-triathlon in a decent time with no prior triathlon training or preparation!

How do you feel about using nutritional supplements?

I believe everyone should supplement their diet with a protein powder and anti-oxidant vitamins and minerals.

What is your nutritional philosophy? Do you have a "power" food?

You are what you eat. The way you look and feel is 85% dependent on what you fuel your body with. My power food is consuming the proper amount of water, carbs, protein, and calories beginning a few days prior to an event.

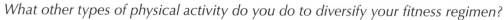

What other types of physical activity do you do to diversify your fitness regimen?

I take kickboxing and plyometrics classes twice a week, spinning classes and cycling outdoors, hip-hop classes, weekend hikes in the Santa Monica mountains, and even conquer the Sand Dune Park for a really tough cardio session.

How do you reward yourself after a great workout?

A liter of cold water.

How does being physically fit affect your confidence?

No one can ever guess my age! Not only does my physique stay young, my skin and eyes stay youthful. I think my healthy lifestyle is responsible for that. Talk about a confidence booster! The cliché, "age ain't nothin' but a number," is *so* true!

www.afadhli.com

Toning and Shaping

Congratulations, you are no longer a beginner! By maintaining your fitness regimen, you have surpassed the efforts of more than 80 percent of the population. You should already see some fairly substantial changes taking place in your physique. It is important to realize, though, that you have only scratched the surface of your genetic potential. Your journey to physique heaven has really just begun. In this phase, you will begin to shape and refine the muscle that you have amassed.

The toning and shaping phase of this system is your entrée into bodysculpting. You have already built a physical foundation; you must now concentrate on erecting a frame. This entails bringing your body into aesthetic proportion and creating symmetry among your muscles. Each muscle group should flow into the next, creating balanced lines that complement one another. You should begin to assess your strengths and weaknesses to become tuned in to the intricacies of your body.

This phase incorporates several changes to further your results. For one, the total volume of exercises and sets that you perform for each muscle group will increase. This allows you to work a muscle more intensively, improving your prospects for shape and tone. Accordingly, your muscles need a longer recuperation period to repair the effects of this added stress. Thus, you'll split your workout into two parts: you'll train half your body in one workout and the other half in the next workout. The net effect is that you'll train each muscle group three times every two weeks (instead of three times a week, as in the body-conditioning routine), giving your body twice as much recuperation as before.

On average, expect to remain in this phase for at least six months. Continue to be patient about your expectations for improving your physique. As previously noted, this program works in a systematic fashion. You'll make gains on a steady, if not spectacular, basis. Therefore, don't attempt to progress to the next level before you are physically and mentally ready for the challenge. Doing so will invariably inhibit your long-term progress.

As always, you should warm up thoroughly before each training session. Because you will work only half of your body each session, be sure to warm up the specific muscles that you will be training. This routine is substantially more intense than the previous one, so an adequate warm-up is imperative to prevent injury.

After your warm-up, go directly to the weight-training portion of your program. As your fitness goals and capabilities evolve, you must adapt your routine to meet your changing needs. This is the only way you can move forward and avoid reaching a training plateau.

Toning and Shaping Protocol

In order to get the most out of the toning and shaping component of this system, adhere to the following protocol:

• **Exercises.** You should use two exercises for each muscle group (as opposed to just one in the body-conditioning routine). This allows you to work your muscles from different angles and lines of pull in the same training session, augmenting your bodysculpting potential. You should use one compound movement and one isolation movement for each muscle group whenever possible. Of course, this is not feasible in the arms, calves, or abdominals because of their anatomic structures. By combining exercises in this way, you stimulate your muscles to their fullest extent.

• **Sets.** You again perform three sets for each exercise. Because you're now using two exercises for each muscle group, you'll perform a total of six sets for each major muscle. (In the body-conditioning routine you performed only three sets.) Initially, this increase in training volume will promote significant muscular fatigue. You should expect to have reduced energy levels for several weeks until your body adapts to this extended workload. Within a short time, though, you'll readily adjust to these demands, and your exercise tolerance will improve dramatically.

• **Rest.** As in the body-conditioning phase, you should rest no more than 30 seconds between sets. Limited rest intervals are one of the primary factors in generating an aerobic effect on your body, and it is paramount to train in an expeditious fashion. Training expeditiously heightens fat burning, bringing out all of your hard-earned muscle tone.

• **Repetitions.** The target repetition number continues to be 15 to 20 reps per set. Using proper form becomes increasingly important at this stage. Because you'll be training with increased intensity, make sure that you don't sacrifice form to complete a set; this will only serve to heighten the potential for injury.

• **Intensity.** The routine uses a progression of intensity in which each successive set requires more effort. As in the body-conditioning routine, your first set should be somewhat challenging. On the second set, you should increase intensity so that you're struggling on the last few reps. Finally, on your third set, you should go all out: by your final repetition, you should reach momentary muscular failure and not be able to do even one more repetition. By the end of your last set, your target muscle should

Toning and Shaping Protocol

Number of exercises:	2 per muscle group
Number of sets:	3 per exercise
Rest between sets:	No more than 30 seconds
Repetitions per set:	15–20
Intensity:	1st set: somewhat challenging
	2nd set: struggling
	3rd set: failure

be completely fatigued, and you should perform your next exercise in the same ladderlike fashion.

The toning and shaping protocol summarizes the specific protocol of the toning and shaping phase of this system. As discussed earlier, you have some discretion in certain aspects of your routine. For the most part, however, you should rigidly follow this protocol to generate optimal results. You are still learning about your body at this point; deviating from the basic protocol can lead to overtraining or injury, setting back your training endeavors.

The Intensity Factor

Perhaps the biggest change between the body-conditioning routine and this routine is an increase in intensity. As a beginner, you were merely building a foundation for your physique. Thus, the intensity of your workout was a less important issue. Because your body was not acclimated to training, working out with too much intensity could have led to overtraining.

If you truly strive to redefine your body, however, you must work harder to get where you want to go. Television commercials that show women with great bodies smiling as they daintily lift weights are pure fantasy. To achieve your full genetic potential, the intensity you apply must exceed your body's work threshold; this is called the *overload principle.* By nature, the human body strives to maintain a stable state of equilibrium called homeostasis. If your training intensity doesn't sufficiently tax your resources, there won't be enough of a stimulus to force your body from its homeostatic state. Only by stressing your muscles beyond their physical capacity can you compel them to produce an adaptive response and exact a change in your body.

You will gradually increase intensity until you are training to momentary muscular failure. From a training perspective, failure equals success! When you first attempt to train to failure, it can be an enlightening experience one that you might not be prepared to endure. While lifting a weight, most women are prone to give up mentally before their muscles truly give out. They may think they have induced muscular failure, yet their muscles are capable of completing several more repetitions. To obtain the best results, you must learn to differentiate between mental failure and physical failure. Remember the adage, "What doesn't kill you makes you stronger." Pushing yourself to the limit will show your internal and external strength and allow your body to achieve more than you ever could have imagined.

To ready your body for the increase in intensity, this routine uses a set progression for muscular acclimation. Your first two sets will prepare you for your final, all-out set. Each set is more intense, until you reach momentary muscular failure on your last set. Because you don't have another set for which to save your energy, you can push yourself to the limit without worrying about preserving your strength reserves. When I train a client, I use the motto, "Last set, best set!" meaning that you should expend all your resources in completing your final set. By progressively adapting your workload, you'll have ample endurance to push hard without overtraining your body.

Of course, along with this increase in intensity, you should expect to experience more mental and physical discomfort. Although most of us seek to avoid discomfort, it is unfortunately an unavoidable and necessary by-product of the training process. Intense training places significant stress on your muscles and taxes your entire nervous system. This in itself produces an uncomfortable effect on your

INTENSITY

In bodysculpting, intensity refers to effort: it is defined as the amount of work performed in a given time. You can heighten intensity in two ways: by increasing the weight you use or by decreasing the rest interval between sets. High-Energy Fitness uses a target rest interval of approximately 30 seconds between sets—a fast training pace by any standard. This elevates your heart rate to optimize fat burning while allowing enough time for your body to recover and generate sufficient intensity for the next set.

Once you progress in your bodysculpting endeavors, High-Energy Fitness mandates that you train to muscular failure. This means that the last repetition of a set should be extremely difficult, if not impossible, to perform. Weight training is one of the few activities in which failure is a desired outcome. This is a strange concept to grasp. We live in a society that rewards us for our accomplishments and punishes us for our failures. From the time we are born, we are urged to succeed. We think of failure as an unacceptable alternative. But in this system, weight training is a means to an end. Your goal should be not to attain a given number of repetitions but to develop a lean, toned physique. Training to failure in the High-Energy Fitness system exacts maximal stress on a muscle while initiating an aerobic effect on the body. This promotes the dual benefit of burning fat while improving muscular shape and hardness.

One of the side benefits of this approach is that it dramatically decreases the amount of time that you need to train. Only a few sets of an exercise are required to produce maximal muscular stress. Once you completely overload a muscle, additional training becomes superfluous. With its rapid training pace, High-Energy Fitness is an efficient method for expediting gains with a minimal commitment of time: the entire workout should be completed in less than an hour.

body. As you approach muscular failure, your body produces a substance called lactic acid that not only brings about muscular fatigue but also causes a burning sensation in the muscles you are training. Your body is likely to quiver as you struggle to complete your final reps. (This is caused by your Golgi tendon reflex threshold, which is a protective response to muscular overload.) All of these responses act against your mental will, challenging you to give up.

When these physiological responses occur, you must be mentally strong enough to think beyond your discomfort. The pain endured while training is short-lived; it subsides within seconds of completing your set. Thus, when training to failure, rationalize that the discomfort will be over momentarily. Realize that once your set is complete, you'll have the satisfaction of setting yourself on a course to achieve the body of your dreams. It's a case of sacrificing short-term satisfaction for long-term gain—a worthy payoff!

Creating a Toning and Shaping Routine

Now that the protocols have been established, you may be wondering about the best way to implement them into a structured training regimen. You can combine exercises for different muscle groups into a practical split routine in many different ways. One possibility is exercising agonist and antagonist muscle groups in the same session. Agonist and antagonist muscle groups are those whose actions directly oppose each another. For example, the biceps and triceps are an agonist–antagonist pair of muscles. When you contract (shorten) your biceps by flexing your arm, your triceps works in an opposing fashion, limiting the contraction. Because blood flow to this entire area is centralized, combining exercises for these muscles in the same workout can increase the benefits of vascular circulation.

Table 4.1 illustrates sample routines that combine agonist and antagonist muscle groups into a cohesive format. Remember that these sample routines are only a guide. Feel free to vary your routine each time you work out.

TABLE 4.1 SAMPLE ROUTINES COMBINING EXERCISES FOR AGONIST AND ANTAGONIST MUSCLE GROUPS

DAY 1: BICEPS, TRICEPS, QUADRICEPS, HAMSTRINGS

WORKOUT 1	WORKOUT 2	WORKOUT 3
Seated dumbbell curl	Standing EZ curl	Cable curl
Preacher curl	Concentration curl	Prone incline curl
Triceps press-down	Two-arm overhead cable extension	One-arm overhead dumbbell extension
Overhead rope extension	Triceps kickback	Triceps dip
Leg press	Lunge	Squat
Front kick	Sissy squat	Leg extension
Stiff-legged dead lift	Seated leg curl	Lying leg curl
Standing cable leg curl	Hyperextension	Good morning

DAY 2: CHEST, BACK, SHOULDERS, CALVES, ABS

WORKOUT 1	WORKOUT 2	WORKOUT 3
Incline dumbbell press	Flat machine press	Push-up
Pec deck flye	Cable crossover	Incline dumbbell flye
Front lat pulldown	Chin-up	Reverse lat pull-down
Seated row	One-arm dumbbell row	Dumbbell pullover
Dumbbell shoulder press	Arnold press	Machine shoulder press
Lateral raise	Bent lateral raise	Upright row
Standing calf raise	Donkey calf raise	Toe press
Seated calf raise	One-leg seated calf raise	Seated calf raise
Crunch	Seated rope crunch	Rope crunch
Hanging leg raise	Reverse crunch	Twisting crunch

Frequency of Ab Training

You might have noticed that I advocate training the abdominals with the same frequency as every other muscle complex—a recommendation that comes as a shock to many women. After all, the majority of fitness professionals advocate daily abdominal exercise. They claim that the abs are an "endurance muscle" and therefore can tolerate more frequent training.

The truth is, however, that your abs aren't structurally different from the other major muscles of your body. The rectus abdominis (the "six-pack" muscle) actually comprises roughly equal amounts of fast-twitch (strength-related) and slow-twitch (endurance-related) fibers, a composition similar to the muscle of the thighs and arms. Compare this to a true endurance-related muscle like the soleus (one of the calf muscles) and you'll see that the abs are just as oriented to strength as they are to endurance.

Moreover, the abdominals are worked indirectly while training other muscle groups. Many fitness professionals overlook this fact. Exercises such as triceps press-downs, lat pull-downs, and squats use the abdominals as stabilizer muscles. Training with the High-Energy Fitness system provides a substantial amount of secondary stress to the abdominal muscles every time you work out. I have worked with many women who had trained their abdominals every day for years.

After cutting the volume of their training and employing proper intensity to their efforts, they substantially improved the appearance of their midsection.

Thus, you should work your abdominals just as you would any other muscle group, focusing on the quality, not the quantity, of training. If you don't feel that you're achieving desired results, examine your training methods instead of adding extra sets or increasing training frequency. Moreover, remember that if you have excess body fat in this area, you will never see the muscle that you have worked so hard to build!

Optimizing Results in the Toning and Shaping Phase

In the toning and shaping phase, it's generally better to work your upper body before training your legs. Your lower body will be fatigued and perhaps slightly unstable immediately after intense training. Thus, it can be difficult for your legs to support your body during many exercises performed in the standing position. This restricts your upper-body work to seated movements. Moreover, because of the large amount of muscle mass involved, leg training tends to sap your energy reserves. By training your lower body at the end of your routine, you get more from your upper-body efforts without significantly affecting your leg workout.

Another important goal in this phase of training is creating aesthetic balance in your proportions. As previously mentioned, you should be in tune with the overall symmetry of your physique and how each muscle complements the others. One side of your body is probably stronger or better developed than the other side (your right biceps might be stronger than your left, your left hamstring might have more muscle than your right, and so forth), causing asymmetrical development. Although your genes play a major role in determining symmetry, external factors can also affect your proportions. For example, women often carry their pocket books on a certain side, increasing their strength on that side at the expense of the other. Bringing both sides of your body into alignment is an important concern.

Furthermore, you should now increase the use of dumbbells and one-arm cable exercises. These movements require each side of your body to perform an equal amount of work (as opposed to movements using barbells and machines, in which your stronger side tends to compensate for your weaker side). Using one-limb movements helps to balance development, not only between different muscle groups, but also between each side of your body. Over time, this will bring your entire physique into harmony.

Finally, you should begin to incorporate supersets into your routine. A superset comprises two consecutive exercises with no rest between them. Supersets further increase workout intensity and, because of the limited rest intervals, increase fat burning.

In this routine, each superset counts as two sets, speeding up the pace of your workout. A muscle begins to recuperate several seconds after the completion of a set. Thus, in a superset, you should attempt to move from one exercise to the other expeditiously. Several different combinations can create an effective superset. Following are some of the better ones:

• A particularly effective superset links a compound movement with an isolation movement. Some examples of supersets using this arrangement are leg presses with leg extensions for the quads, incline presses with pec deck flyes for

■ Make sure you have completed all phases of toning before proceeding to bodysculpting.

the chest, and shoulder presses with lateral raises for the shoulders.

• Unweighted exercises also work well in supersets, especially for the legs. You can train to failure on a weighted movement and still have enough energy to make it through an unweighted leg exercise. Some examples of supersets combining weighted and unweighted movements are leg presses with sissy squats, front squats with walking lunges, and stiff-legged dead lifts with hyperextensions.

• Agonist and antagonist muscle groups are another excellent combination for supersets. Some examples are biceps with triceps (cable-rope hammer curls with nosebreakers, incline curls with overhead rope extensions), chest with back (incline dumbbell presses with lat pull-downs, flat flyes with seated rows), and quadriceps with hamstrings (hack squats with lying leg curls, front squats with reverse hyperextensions).

Unilateral (one-arm or one-leg) movements do not translate well into supersets. Exercises performed unilaterally provide too much rest for the side that is not active, thereby decreasing the benefit of a superset. Thus, exercises like concentration curls and one-arm dumbbell rows are poor choices for inclusion in a superset. Experiment with various combinations, trying different supersets for each muscle group. As with all facets of training, variation is a key to achieving results.

When to Advance to the Next Level

When you feel that you are ready to take the final step and undertake targeted bodysculpting, you should first consider several points. Because this is a progressive system, you again will have to increase your intensity of effort to secure results. You should meet the following provisions before going forward:

1. Make sure that you have mastered all the High-Energy Fitness principles and concepts. Understanding fitness should be second nature at this point. You should have a clear grasp of all training fundamentals. It is not enough to have an overview of these factors; they must be ingrained. Targeted bodysculpting cannot be carried out if you're still learning your way.

2. Make sure that you have accomplished the objectives of this phase of training. The toning and shaping routine is intended to create the basis on which to apply advanced bodysculpting techniques. If you are still in the rudimentary stages of developing your physique, continuing with this routine will better help

you achieve long-term progress. You should not try to run before you are able to walk; doing so is bound to make you fall.

3. Make sure that you are willing and able to push yourself to the limit. The increase in intensity and effort will be even greater than before. Targeted bodysculpting is for those who desire to maximize their bodies' potential. If this is your aim, you must be willing to do the work required to reach those heights. You should be able to move through the toning and shaping routine easily, feeling both mentally and physically capable to go beyond your current training pace. If you cannot do this, the advanced routine will be too intense.

If you have any doubts about whether you meet these prerequisites, continue with the toning and shaping routine until you are ready to move forward. Don't feel that there is a time limit for your progress or even that you must ever take the next step. You can acquire an excellent physique using this toning and shaping phase, and depending on your expectations and goals, you might be content to continue with it indefinitely. But if you aspire to reach your ultimate potential, you need to take the final step. If this is your mission, the next chapter will help you realize your fitness dreams!

Targeted Bodysculpting

You must have a strong desire to rise to the challenge of sculpting your body to its ultimate potential. Training at a level that optimizes your shape and symmetry requires tremendous effort. The further you progress in your fitness endeavors, the more difficult it is to improve your physique. You can achieve roughly 90 percent of your potential by adhering to the toning and shaping phase of this system; the remaining 10 percent is what separates the good from the extraordinary. If you are prepared to meet this challenge, the targeted bodysculpting phase of the High-Energy Fitness system will take you all the way to physique heaven!

You should, at this point, possess a shapely, toned physique that needs only some fine tuning. Your goals are now probably lofty: maybe you want to look your best in a slinky dress or bikini or perhaps you even have aspirations to become a fitness competitor. Whatever your desires, you control your destiny. You can shape specific muscles in various ways to create balanced, aesthetic proportions. Consider yourself a sculptor and your body an unfinished statue in need of some finishing touches. This is where bodysculpting becomes both a science and an art.

The advanced phase of this system is the essence of High-Energy Fitness: a merging of mind and muscle to achieve physical perfection. To help you sculpt your body perfect, the routine now is split into three parts, and you perform more exercises and sets per muscle group. Because the volume of training is greater and exercise intensity increases, your muscles will need more recuperation. Thus, you will train each muscle group only once per week (as volume and intensity increase, frequency must decrease).

Because there are nine categories of major muscles, you can split your routine by training three muscle groups each workout. I recommend the following combination as an effective training split:

- Day 1: Chest, back, abdominals
- Day 2: Quadriceps, hamstrings, calves
- Day 3: Shoulders, biceps, triceps

This combination works all the major muscles and allows for excellent rest and recuperation of synergistic muscle groups. Of course, alternative ways of splitting your routine can be equally effective. There is no best method for combining muscle groups into a routine. Don't be afraid to experiment with different combinations to see what works best for you.

Targeted Bodysculpting Protocol

In order to get the most out of the targeted bodysculpting component of this system, adhere to the following protocol:

- **Exercises.** You should use from two to four exercises for each major muscle group, and, as always, vary your routine as much as possible. At this level, you should selectively combine the exercises to best sculpt your proportions. Several exercise variables affect your bodysculpting results, including the angle of pull in a movement, the amount of stretch applied to the target muscle, the positioning of your hands or feet, and the ability to isolate a specific muscle. Considering these factors, I have indexed the exercises by groups that work synergistically with one another. By combining the exercises as specified in the upcoming chapters, you can optimize the shape of each muscle complex. You should normally choose at least one exercise from each group. But if you want to pay special heed to a certain area and add a second movement, feel free to do so. Also, although it is normally better to train larger muscle complexes at the beginning of your workout, you should prioritize lagging muscles by training them first. In this way, you'll have more energy to train those muscles and will derive better results from your efforts.

Bodysculpting Protocol

Number of exercises: 2–4 per muscle group

Number of sets: 2–4 per exercise

Rest between sets: No more than 30 seconds (as few as 8 for selected groups)

Intensity: Failure on all sets (reduced intensity for overdeveloped muscle groups)

- **Sets.** You should perform anywhere from 6 to 12 sets per muscle group, 2 to 4 sets per exercise. Because larger muscles have a greater capacity for work, they can endure more total sets than smaller muscle groups. Moreover, smaller muscles receive secondary stress in many exercises (for example, the arms during most upper-body work and the hamstrings in various compound leg movements), further reducing the need for additional sets. Table 5.1 details the approximate number of sets that you can perform for each muscle group. At the advanced level, High-Energy Fitness is very intense, so I advise you to start on the lower end of the recommended range. Being overzealous can lead to overtraining, which will retard your progress. As you move forward, assess your results and add additional sets as needed.

- **Rest.** As in the lower-level routines, keep rest intervals to no more than 30 seconds between sets. If definition is your aim, keep rest intervals as short as you can because this increases both the immediate aerobic effect and EPOC. Employing supersets and giant sets (discussed on page 38) will heighten this effect, thereby maximizing fat-burning capacity.

- **Repetitions.** The target number of repetitions remains 15 to 20 per set. You can, however, selectively use fewer repetitions where appropriate. If you want to add size to a specific muscle group to bring your body into proportion, use fewer

TABLE 5.1 NUMBER OF SETS PER MUSCLE GROUP

MUSCLE GROUP	SETS
Back	9–12
Chest	8–10
Shoulders	8–10
Triceps	6–9
Biceps	6–9
Quadriceps	9–12
Hamstrings and glutes	8–10
Calves	6–9
Abdominals	6–9

reps for that particular muscle group (in the range of 8 to 12 repetitions). Again, make sure to train with good form, and apply continuous tension to your muscles throughout each repetition.

- **Intensity.** After a sufficient warm-up, you should perform all sets at or near momentary muscular failure, the point at which you can't physically complete another rep. If you feel that a certain muscle group is overdeveloped, you should train it at a reduced intensity. Never discontinue training a muscle, though. This will ensure that you maintain a degree of "hardness" in the area and avoid developing significant strength imbalances between agonist and antagonist muscle groups.

The bodysculpting protocol on page 36 summarizes the specific protocol for the targeted bodysculpting phase. This protocol has endured the test of time. Thousands of women have used it successfully to redefine their bodies. As previously noted, however, this phase is dynamic, and you should adapt the stated guidelines to your physique and abilities. Within the framework of this system, endeavor to turn your body into a masterpiece!

Creating a Targeted Bodysculpting Routine

In the targeted bodysculpting phase, the system is more flexible, allowing you to customize the routine to your individual needs. The art of bodysculpting is specific to each individual and ultimately subject to your concept of the ideal female physique. It is sometimes difficult to see yourself as you really are, and women often have a distorted opinion of their own bodies. Therefore, you should try to look at yourself objectively, as if you were evaluating the physique of another woman. When you are in tune with your body, you can make intelligent decisions about improving your deficiencies.

Before constructing your specific routine, you should assess your physique to choose a course of action. Although you cannot change your genes, you have substantial control over the shape of your physique. Bodysculpting gives you the ability to alter your proportions significantly, creating a balanced, symmetrical body. For instance, if you have a naturally blocky waist, there is no way to change this fact (short of radical surgery). Although you can reduce fat in this area, your waist will still have a blocky appearance. However, by employing bodysculpting techniques to add muscle to your medial deltoid and upper-back areas, you

REPETITIONS

You can use a variety of repetition ranges to achieve your fitness goals. The following rules apply to repetition ranges:

- A program using 4 to 6 repetitions (a low rep range) is best for increasing strength and power. This range is oriented to powerlifting goals.
- A program using 8 to 12 repetitions (a moderate rep range) is best for increasing overall muscularity. This range is good for developing a bodybuilder's physique.
- A program using 15 to 20 repetitions (a high rep range) is best for improving muscular endurance. This range is good for achieving lean muscle tone without significantly increasing muscular bulk.

The speed at which to perform repetitions is also an area of debate. Controversy exists among fitness professionals about the best speed at which to perform a repetition. Studies conducted on this subject have been largely inconclusive. In the High-Energy Fitness system, how fast you perform a repetition is relatively unimportant as long as you follow the ABCs of lifting: always be in control! Make sure that your target muscle directs each repetition; allow the muscle to move the weight during both the positive and negative phases of the movement. Momentum or gravity should never dictate the speed of a repetition. Use a smooth, consistent motion to ensure complete stimulation of your target muscles and to reduce the possibility of injury.

It is also beneficial to perform repetitions rhythmically. Each repetition should flow into the next, creating a distinct tempo for the set. This helps to set a training "groove," making it easier to target the proper muscles.

increase your shoulder-to-waist differential. This gives the illusion of your having a smaller waist and the classic hourglass physique. Bodysculpting is all about illusion. With proper knowledge and effort, you can mask your genetic limitations.

In subsequent chapters, I discuss the nine major muscle groups and examine the bodysculpting possibilities for each area. Exercises are grouped to show you how to combine movements for maximal effect. State-of-the-art training tips explain how to optimize performance. Finally, sample routines are presented to illustrate the possibilities for crafting an exciting, customized routine. Choose one exercise from each group (for example, in Chapter 6 you could choose chest dip from group 1, incline dumbbell flye from group 2, and pec deck flye from group 3), then select one of the four workouts described to focus on what you're looking for in a bodysculpting routine.

Optimizing Results in the Targeted Bodysculpting Phase

You should now begin to employ giant sets in your workout. A giant set incorporates three or more different exercises in succession, without rest between them (as opposed to a superset, which uses two sequential exercises). A superset equals two sets; a giant set counts as three (or more) sets. By performing three or more exercises consecutively, you are able to generate more intensity than you can with supersets. Because exercises are performed in rapid succession, you achieve considerable aerobic effect and enhanced EPOC, factors that accelerate fat burning. Giant sets are thus particularly effective for heightening muscular definition.

To get the most out of a giant set, it is best to choose exercises that require alternative angles or different muscular actions in the performance of the movement (as outlined in my exercise groupings). For example, an excellent combination for a giant set of the abdominals is the crunch, reverse curl, and jackknife: the crunch focuses on the upper abdominal region, the reverse curl targets the lower portion of the abs, and the jackknife works the obliques. Although these movements all stress the abdominal musculature, they complement each other to produce a sum greater than their parts.

To apply advanced bodysculpting techniques correctly, you must have a clear grasp of muscular anatomy. In the beginning stages of High-Energy Fitness, when your bodysculpting capabilities were limited, it was enough to have merely a general awareness of this information. To take your physique to its ultimate potential, however, you should now understand how each muscle affects your proportions. I recommend that you look over the anatomical diagrams in chapter 1 (see pages 6 and 7) and study the position and proximity of the various muscles. If you're really adventurous, you might want to pick up a textbook on anatomy; the knowledge procured will benefit you greatly in your bodysculpting endeavors.

Allison Bookless

My story: I am a full-time firefighter and paramedic. I need to be physically fit to do my job. It takes a lot of specific training to be able to do well in the physical agility test.

Achievements: 2000 1st Place Winner NPC Team Universe, 2000 Champion Overall NPC Debbie Kruck Classic

What motivated you to begin a weight-training program? How old were you when you started?

I was 12 years old. I started because my diving coach wanted us to become stronger and better athletes.

How do you feel about using nutritional supplements?

Nutritional supplementation is a must, however nothing beats a good diet!

Do you have a "power" food?

I love green veggies! They make me feel so healthy—and I drink a ton of water.

What other types of physical activity do you do to diversify your fitness regimen?

Running, snowboarding, adventure races, gymnastics, swimming, biking . . .

©www.regbradford.com

How do you reward yourself after a great workout?

The workout is the reward. I feel wonderful after I give 110% in the gym. My husband rewards me with a gift certificate for a massage!

Do you have any training tips you'd like to pass on?

Do everything in moderation. It won't happen overnight so patience is a must. Put a picture on the frig to help motivate you—it can be a saying or a person.

www.allisonbookless.com

Sexy Chest

Many women covet pert, shapely breasts. Unfortunately, breast tissue often heads south as you grow older, succumbing to the effects of gravity, pregnancy, and age. "How can I prevent my breasts from sagging?" is one of the most common questions I am asked. Although training your chest will not change the overall structure of your breasts (breast tissue is fat, and, as previously discussed, you cannot shape fat), it can help to prevent them from drooping by firming the surrounding muscles of the breastbone. This provides a distinct lift to your breasts, helping to offset the ravages of time.

Moreover, although it won't beef up your bustline, training can create the illusion of a fuller, sexier chest. Rather than seeking a surgical solution to pump up your breasts, you can train to secure a natural edge. For instance, developing the inner aspect of your chest suggests more cleavage; building the upper portion of your chest makes your breasts appear more ample. As the sculptor, you have the power to shape your chest any way you choose.

Bodysculpting Routine

The chest muscle fibers have a sunburst appearance. With attachments at three different bones—the breastbone (sternum), collarbone (clavicle), and upper arm (humerus)—these muscle fibers run in many directions. Because of this unique structure, the pectorals can benefit from exercises that use a variety of angles. Exercises for the chest are classified into compound and isolation movements. Additional attention is given to an exercise's ability to provide tension at various points throughout a movement.

• **Group 1**—presses, push-ups, chest dips, and similar variations. These compound movements stress the pectorals as well as many secondary muscles. They help to develop fullness in the region and strengthen the surrounding musculature, giving the breasts maximum support. By varying the bench angle, you can shift the emphasis of the movement to the upper, middle, or lower portions of the chest.

• **Group 2**—dumbbell flyes and similar variations. These isolation movements work the chest in the body's horizontal plane. Because of gravitational pull,

ANGLES

A muscle is made up of thousands and thousands of tiny, threadlike fibers. When properly executed, a weighted exercise targets specific fibers within a muscle or group of muscles. Each exercise, however, hits only a portion of the fibers in these muscles. Although certain exercises stimulate a greater number of muscle fibers than others, it is beneficial to use a variety of exercises that work a muscle from different angles. By using a multi-angled approach, you'll ultimately stress all of the fibers in a muscle and thereby develop your physique to its fullest.

After you become experienced at training, you might decide to use certain exercise angles more frequently than others to accentuate lagging muscle groups. You can, for instance, choose exercises that focus on the upper chest, side deltoids, or inner thighs. This can aid the bodysculpting process by helping to bring individual muscles into proportion with one another. But realize that this is not an exact science. Although an exercise can exert more stress on specific fibers within a muscle, it commonly involves other areas of the same muscle (and perhaps secondary muscles too) to some degree. Thus, to get the most out of your efforts, it is important to understand the limitations of each muscle group and to apply bodysculpting techniques accordingly.

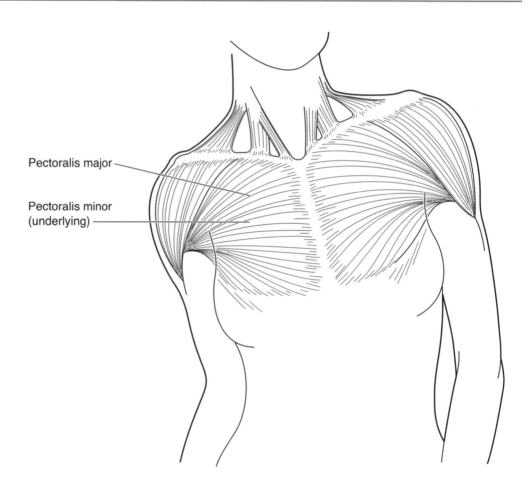

Pectoralis major

Pectoralis minor
(underlying)

■ Muscles of the chest.

they require great force at the beginning portion of the move. As you bring the weight up, however, the stress gradually diminishes up to the finish position, where muscular tension is virtually nonexistent. Thus, to maximize results, it is imperative to focus on the first half of each rep, making sure to get a nice stretch at the bottom. But don't allow your arms to stretch significantly below parallel with the floor; doing so places undue stress on the shoulder joint, potentially causing serious injury.

• **Group 3**—pec deck flyes, crossovers, and similar variations. These isolation movements help to give a polished look to the pectoral region. Because they provide continuous tension throughout the course of the move, an intense contraction can be achieved at the finish position. Hence, by forcefully squeezing your pecs together at peak contraction, you can recruit muscle fibers that are difficult to activate in free-weight exercises.

Bodysculpting Tips

1. The three basic angles that you can use in chest training (incline, flat, and decline) emphasize different portions of the pecs. An incline exercise accentuates the upper chest, flat works the middle portion, and decline stresses the lower region. By assessing the symmetry of your chest, you can selectively use these angles to augment your proportions.

2. The upper pectoral region has the greatest impact on the appearance of your chest, making incline exercises of primary importance. When properly developed, this area gives the appearance of a firm, elevated chest. For best results, keep the angle on incline exercises between 30 and 40 degrees. Using a steeper angle excessively activates the anterior deltoids, taking stress away from the chest muscles.

3. The lower pectoral region tends to be the easiest portion to develop and therefore needs little direct stimulation in most instances. Further, a woman's anatomical structure makes developing this area of limited utility. Thus, unless the lower portion of the chest is a specific weak spot, use decline exercises sparingly, mostly for variety.

4. Push-ups can be a great complementary exercise, either as an alternative to chest presses or when combined with other movements in a superset or giant set. Depending on your body weight, you may find these exercises difficult to execute. If you have trouble performing military push-ups, start by using the modified position (from your knees). Gradually attempt to perform the exercise military style until you're able to perform a full set this way.

TABLE 6.1   EXERCISES FOR THE CHEST

GROUP	EXERCISES
Group 1	Chest dip
	Incline dumbbell press
	Flat dumbbell press
	Incline machine press
	Push-up
Group 2	Flat dumbbell flye
	Incline dumbbell flye
	Decline dumbbell flye
Group 3	High cable crossover
	One-arm cable crossover
	Low cable crossover
	Pec deck flye

TABLE 6.2   SAMPLE TARGETED WORKOUTS FOR THE CHEST

WORKOUT	IN THE GYM		AT HOME	
	Exercise	**Sets**	**Exercise**	**Sets**
1	Incline dumbell press (p. 46)	2	Push-up (p. 48) supersetted with incline dumbbell flye (p. 50)	3
	Flat dumbbell flye (p. 49) supersetted with push-up (p. 48)	2	Low cable crossover (p. 54)	3
	Pec deck flye (p. 55)	3		
2	Incline machine press (p. 47) supersetted with decline dumbbell flye (p. 51)	3	Flat dumbbell press (p. 56)	3
	High cable crossover (p. 52)	2	Incline dumbbell flye (p. 50)	3
			One-arm cable crossover (p. 53)	3
3	Flat dumbbell press (p. 56) supersetted with incline dumbbell flye (p. 50)	3		
	Low cable crossover (p. 54)	3		
4	Chest dip (p. 45)	2		
	Incline dumbbell press (p. 46)	2		
	Flat dumbbell flye (p. 49)	3		
	One-arm cable crossover (p. 53)	3		

CHEST DIP

Because the chest dip requires lifting your own body weight, it is a difficult move for most women. But if you can build up the strength to perform it, the results are worth it! Begin by grasping the bars on a parallel bar apparatus with your palms turned in. Bend your legs to a 90-degree angle, cross your ankles, and tilt your upper body forward, with your hips to the back. Maintaining a distinct forward tilt, slowly bend your elbows and lower your body as far as comfortably possible. Return to the start position.

INCLINE DUMBBELL PRESS

The incline dumbbell press is my favorite move for developing the upper chest. Begin by lying face up on an incline bench, planting your feet firmly on the floor. Grasp two dumbbells, and with your palms facing away from your body, bring them to shoulder level so that they rest just above your armpits. Simultaneously press both dumbbells directly over your chest, moving them in toward each other on the ascent. At the finish of the movement, the sides of the dumbbells should gently touch together. Feel a contraction in your chest muscles, and then slowly reverse direction, returning to the start position.

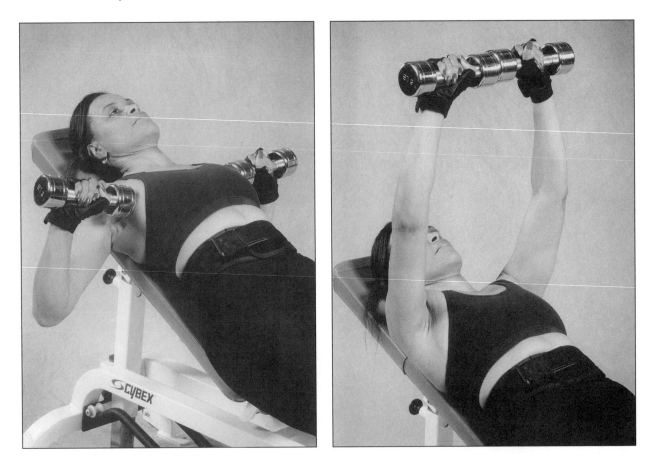

INCLINE MACHINE PRESS

Begin by sitting in an incline chest-press machine, aligning your upper chest with the handles on the machine. Grasp the handles with a shoulder-width grip, keeping your palms facing away from your body. Slowly press the handles forward, stopping just before you fully lock your elbows. Feel a contraction in your chest muscles at the finish of the movement, and then slowly reverse direction and return to the start position.

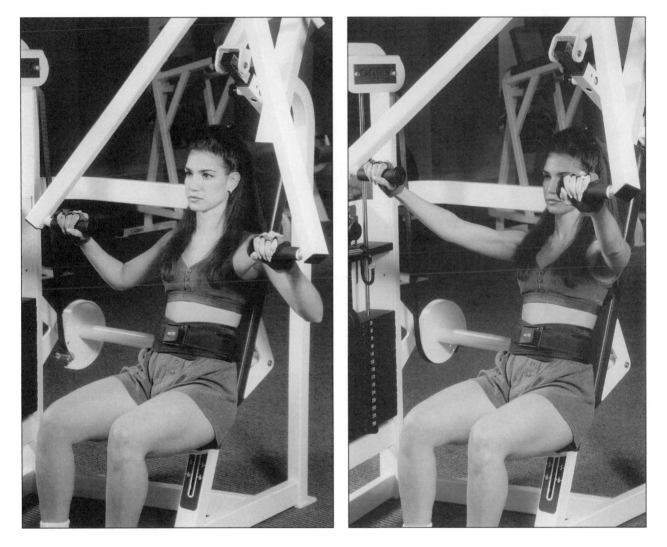

PUSH-UP

The push-up is a terrific alternative to chest-press exercises and has the added benefit of convenience; you can perform the move almost anywhere! Begin with your hands and toes on the floor. Your torso and legs should remain rigid; keep your back perfectly straight throughout the move. Bend your arms and slowly lower your body, stopping just before your chest touches the ground. Feel a stretch in your chest muscles, and then reverse direction, pushing your body up along the same path back to the start position.

FLAT DUMBBELL FLYE

Begin by lying back on a flat bench, planting your feet firmly on the floor. Grasp two dumbbells and bring them out to your sides, maintaining a slight bend to your elbows throughout the move. Your palms should be facing in and toward the ceiling, and your upper arms should be roughly even with the height of the bench. Slowly raise the weights upward in a semicircular motion, as if you were hugging a large tree. Gently touch the weights together at the top of the move, and after feeling a contraction in your chest muscles, slowly return the weights along the same path to the start position.

INCLINE DUMBBELL FLYE

Begin by lying back on an incline bench set at approximately 30 to 40 degrees, planting your feet firmly on the floor. Grasp two dumbbells and bring them out to your sides, maintaining a slight bend of your elbows throughout the move. Your palms should be facing in and toward the ceiling, and your upper arms should be roughly parallel with the level of the bench. Slowly raise the weights upward in a circular motion, as if you were hugging a large tree. Gently touch the weights together at the top of the move, and after feeling a contraction in your chest muscles, slowly return the weights along the same path to the start position.

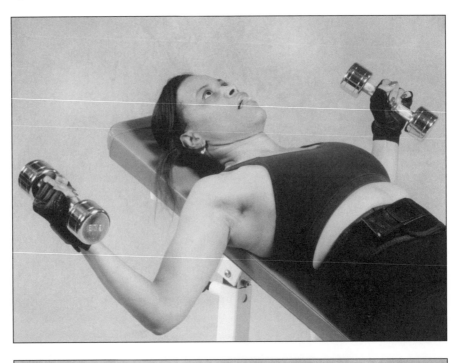

DECLINE DUMBBELL FLYE

Lie on a bench set at a moderate decline. Grasp two dumbbells and hold them to your sides, slightly bending your elbows. Your palms should be turned in and toward the ceiling, your upper arms roughly parallel with the bench. Slowly raise the weights in a circular motion, as if hugging a large tree. Gently touch the weights at the top of the move, and after feeling a contraction in your chest, return to the start position.

HIGH CABLE CROSSOVER

Begin by grasping the handles of an overhead pulley apparatus (cable crossover machine). Stand with your feet about shoulder-width apart and your torso bent slightly forward at the waist. Slowly pull both handles downward and across your body in a semicircular movement. Bring your hands together at the level of your hips and squeeze your chest muscles so that you feel a contraction in the chest area. Then, slowly reverse direction, allowing your hands to return along the same path to the start position.

ONE-ARM CABLE CROSSOVER

This movement allows you to really concentrate on each side of your chest. Begin by grasping the handle of an overhead pulley (cable crossover machine) with your left hand. Stand with your feet about shoulder-width apart and your torso bent slightly forward at the waist. Slowly pull the handle down and across your body in a semicircle. When your hand crosses the midline of your body, squeeze your chest muscles so that you feel a contraction. Then, slowly reverse direction, returning to the start position. Repeat with your right arm after performing the desired number of reps with your left arm. To perform the move at home, attach a strength band to a stationary object and perform the move as described.

At Home

LOW CABLE CROSSOVER

Because the shoulder is flexed during movement, this variation of the crossover targets the upper chest fibers. Begin by grasping the loop handles of a low pulley apparatus (cable crossover machine). Stand with your feet about shoulder-width apart and your torso bent slightly forward at the waist. Slowly pull both handles up and across your body, creating a semicircular movement. Bring your hands together at the level of your hips and squeeze your chest muscles so that you feel a contraction in the cleavage area. Then, slowly reverse direction, allowing your hands to return along the same path to the start position. To perform the move at home, attach a strength band to a stationary object and perform the move as described.

At Home

PEC DECK FLYE

Begin by placing your forearms on the pads of a pec deck machine. Your elbows should be pressed into the pads at all times, and your back should remain immobile throughout the movement. Simultaneously press both pads together, allowing them to gently touch each other directly in front of your chest. Contract your chest muscles, and then slowly reverse direction, returning to the start position.

CHEST EXERCISES

FLAT DUMBBELL PRESS

Due to the freedom of movement this exercise allows, I prefer it to the more popular barbell bench press. Begin by lying face up on a flat bench with your feet planted firmly on the floor. Grasp two dumbbells and, with your palms facing away from your body, bring them to shoulder level so that they rest just above your armpits. Simultaneously press both dumbbells directly over your chest, moving them in toward each other on the ascent. At the finish of the movement, the sides of the dumbbells should gently touch together. Feel a contraction in your chest muscles at the top of the movement and then slowly reverse direction, returning to the start position.

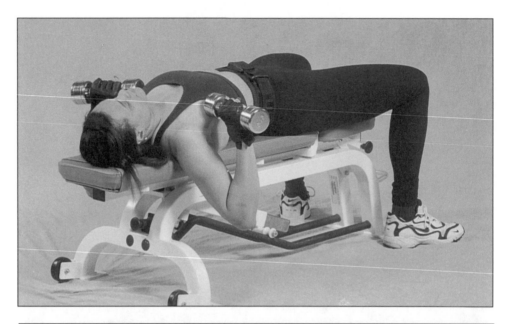

DeeAnn Donovan

My story: Any mother who feels as though their fitness goals and dreams have been put on hold while raising their children should talk to me. I am a mother of three, work full time as a fitness and swimwear model, compete in figure competitions, and am a certified personal trainer.

Achievements: Mrs. New York; International—Title Holder; 2001 NPC Team Universe Figure Championships, 10th Place Finalist; 2001 NPC Bev Francis Atlantic States Figure Championships, 4th place, National Qualifier

©DeeAnn Donovan

How do you do it all?

Proper balance and scheduling! I'm up at 5 A.M., on the treadmill from 5:30–6:30, having breakfast and a shower from 6:30–7:30, 7:30–9:00 I'm getting the kids up and taking them to school, 9:30–10:30 strength training at the gym, and the rest of the day is for shoots, modeling, or whatever else comes up.

How do you feel about using nutritional supplements?

Supplementation is very important. I learned through trial and error (and an empty checkbook!). Everyone is different so it's important to find what works for you. When you're trying supplements, be sure to try one at a time, otherwise you'll never know which is working.

What is your nutritional philosophy? Do you have a "power" food?

I've found that through a diet consisting of high amounts of protein—chicken breasts, turkey, egg whites, and whey protein shakes—I am able to stay very lean and have no problems with water retention. I only eat carbs at breakfast and lunch through oatmeal, broccoli, an apple, or a baked potato. The only fats I eat are in the form of nuts or olive oil. I have found that eating 6 small meals a day and drinking as much water as possible has really been great for my metabolism.

What other types of physical activity do you do to diversify your fitness regimen?

Although the majority of my life is very regimented, with a strict adherence to cardio and strength training routines, it is not unusual to find me rollerblading with the kids, tumbling on the gymnastics mat with my daughter, or playing tennis with my friends on the spur of the moment

How do you reward yourself after a great workout?

I've decided that this is a life mission for me, so instead of subjecting my body and mind to an endless cycle of highs and lows, I try to moderate everything. I won't go to either extreme with my eating habits or rewards. This seems to keep me satisfied all the time. (Although, a big piece of chocolate mousse cake while sitting in the hot tub does appeal to me at times.)

Do you have any weight-training tips to pass on?

Vary your routine and your diet! I'm always switching exercises and intensities and seasoning my foods in different ways. I never do the same thing.

www.deeannmodel.com

Hourglass Back

The back is an area that women tend to neglect. Because these muscles aren't readily apparent when you look in a mirror, it's easy to bypass them in favor of training the muscles on the front of your body. However, a well-sculpted back, in conjunction with nicely rounded shoulders, can help to create the illusion of a small waist. This accentuates the classic hourglass physique. Furthermore, although *you* may have difficulty seeing these muscles, other people certainly can! Rest assured, a nicely detailed back is destined to attract attention in everything from a strapless dress to a swimsuit.

The muscles of your back also play a central role in maintaining good posture. Poor posture causes you to slouch, contributing to a tired, haggard appearance. This makes you look old and enfeebled, which has a profound effect on how others perceive you. Conversely, an erect posture projects a commanding presence, giving you an aura of self-confidence in both your professional and social endeavors.

Bodysculpting Routine

The back is the largest muscle complex in the upper body. Unfortunately, due to anatomical considerations, it's virtually impossible to effectively isolate the individual back muscles. However, by varying the angle of pull in the exercises, you can direct stress to various areas of your back. Therefore, exercises for the back are classified by the performance angles possible.

- **Group 1**—pull-downs, chins, and similar variations. These exercises use an overhead angle that pulls in a line approximately parallel to your body. You can create additional angles by using a straight line of pull (behind-the-neck exercises) or a frontal line of pull (leaning slightly back during performance).

- **Group 2**—rows and similar variations. These exercises employ a perpendicular line of pull and allow you to exert maximum contraction of the scapula (shoulder blades), thus targeting many of the muscles of the inner back. They also permit you to use many one-arm movements with dumbbells and cables, helping to improve your muscular balance and symmetry.

It is important to train every muscle in your body at least once a week. Do not neglect any muscle group, especially in the beginning stages of training. Many women want to focus on trouble areas at the exclusion of training the rest of their bodies. I am often asked, "Why do I need to train my back? I don't care about my back!" The body functions holistically, and muscle groups interrelate in a synergistic fashion. Ignoring certain muscle groups will disrupt the symmetry of your body and hence detract from the aesthetics of your physique. Because agonist and antagonist muscles oppose each other, training one muscle at the exclusion of another will inevitably create a muscular imbalance in your physique. This will alter your muscular function and make you considerably more prone to injury.

- **Group 3**—straight-arm pull-downs, pullovers, and similar variations. These exercises use an arcing motion (shoulder joint extension) that really works the lats. By protracting the scapula, they also activate the muscles that tie in the chest and back, known as the serratus. Although often overlooked, these exercises are an excellent complement to rows and chins and add an extra dimension to a well-constructed back routine.

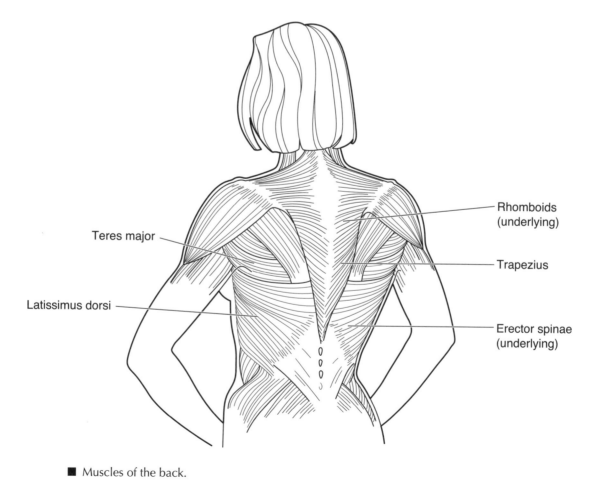

Teres major

Latissimus dorsi

Rhomboids (underlying)

Trapezius

Erector spinae (underlying)

■ Muscles of the back.

Bodysculpting Tips

1. You should vary your hand spacing among narrow, medium, and wide grips. This allows you to work in line with the direction of the fibers of the individual muscles of the back. Do not go more than several inches past a shoulder-width grip on any lat exercise, however. This unnecessarily limits your range of motion, reducing the effectiveness of the movement.

2. Using a reverse grip (palms facing toward you when overhead) on your exercises activates the biceps to a greater degree, thereby reducing stress on the muscles of your back. Many women gravitate to reverse-grip exercises because the secondary influence of the biceps makes them easier to perform. The biceps, however, are much weaker than the back and therefore fatigue before you fully stimulate the target muscles. Thus, you don't receive optimal benefit from the exercise.

If this problem occurs, it can be helpful to use lifting straps when performing movements with a reverse grip. Otherwise, stick to a pronated (palms facing away from you when overhead) or neutral (palms facing one another) grip. Use the reverse grip sparingly, mostly for variety.

3. The best way to optimally develop your inner back is by consciously squeezing your scapula together during exercise performance. To bring out the detail in these muscles, try to make your shoulder blades touch one another on each contraction. Because of the proximity of the back muscles, it often is difficult to acquire a mind-to-muscle link in this area. Hence, extra attention and focus is required to maximize results.

4. It is imperative that you achieve a full stretch on the negative portion of each repetition. Women often shorten the range of motion on back movements, focusing only on the contraction. The stretch, however, lengthens the muscles of the back, which increases both muscular stimulation and upper-body flexibility. Thus, allow the weight to pull slightly on your scapula until you feel a deep stretch in the muscles you are training.

TABLE 7.1 EXERCISES FOR THE BACK

GROUP	EXERCISES
Group 1	Front lat pull-down
	Reverse lat pull-down
	Behind-the-neck lat pull-down
	Chin-up
Group 2	Seated row
	One-arm seated row
	One-arm dumbbell row
	T-bar row
	One-arm standing low row
Group 3	Straight-arm pull-down
	Dumbbell pullover
	Lying cable pullover

TABLE 7.2 SAMPLE TARGETED WORKOUTS FOR THE BACK

WORKOUT	IN THE GYM		AT HOME	
	Exercise	**Sets**	**Exercise**	**Sets**
1	Chin-up (p. 65)	3	Chin-up (p. 65)	3
	One-arm seated row (p. 67)	3	One-arm dumbbell row (p. 68)	4
	Straight-arm pull-down (p. 71)	3	Straight-arm pull-down (p. 71)	3
2	Front lat pull-down (p. 67) supersetted with seated row (p. 66)	3	Chin-up (p. 65)	3
	One-arm dumbbell row (p. 68)		One-arm seated row (p. 67)	4
	Dumbbell pullover (p. 72)	3	Dumbbell pullover (p. 72)	3
3	Reverse lat pull-down (p. 63) supersetted with T-bar row (p. 69)	3		
	One-arm standing low row (p. 70)	3		
	Straight-arm pull-down (p. 71)	3		
4	Behind-the-neck lat pull-down (p. 64)	3		
	One-arm seated row (p. 67)	4		
	Lying cable pullover (p. 73)	3		

FRONT LAT PULL-DOWN

Begin by grasping a straight bar attached to a lat pull-down machine. With your hands shoulder-width apart and palms turned forward, secure your knees under the restraint pad, and fully straighten your arms so you feel a complete stretch in your lats. Maintain a slight backward tilt and arch your lower back through the move. Slowly pull the bar to your upper chest, bringing your elbows back. Squeeze your shoulder blades together and then slowly reverse direction, returning to the start position.

REVERSE LAT PULL-DOWN

It's beneficial to use lifting straps for this exercise to prevent the biceps from fatiguing before the lats. Begin by grasping a lat pull-down bar with your hands shoulder-width apart and your palms turned toward you. Secure your knees under the restraint pad, and fully straighten your arms so you feel a complete stretch in your lats. Maintain a slight backward tilt of your body, and arch your lower back through the move. Slowly pull the bar to your upper chest, bringing your elbows back as you pull. Squeeze your shoulder blades together, and then slowly reverse direction, returning to the start position.

BEHIND-THE-NECK LAT PULL-DOWN

Begin by grasping a straight bar attached to a lat pull-down machine. With your hands shoulder-width apart and your palms turned forward, secure your knees under the restraint pad, and fully straighten your arms so you feel a complete stretch in your lats. Slowly pull the bar down behind your neck, bringing your elbows back as you pull. Squeeze your shoulder blades together, and then slowly reverse direction, returning to the start position. Although this move provides a unique training angle for the back, be careful during performance; it can irritate the shoulder complex and potentially cause injury. If you feel any undue stress in the neck and/or shoulder region, discard the behind-the-neck lat pull-down from your repertoire.

CHIN-UP

Begin by taking a shoulder-width, overhand grip on a chinning bar. Fully straighten your arms so that you feel a complete stretch in your lats. Bend your knees and cross your ankles. Keeping your back arched, slowly pull yourself up until your chin rises above the bar. Contract your lats, and then slowly lower yourself to the start position. If you have trouble performing this exercise, use a Gravitron™ machine (if your gym has one). This excellent device decreases resistance according to your abilities, allowing you to complete the target number of reps.

BACK EXERCISES

SEATED ROW

Begin by grasping a V-bar attached to a low pulley with your palms facing each other. Sit down in front of the pulley with your feet against the footplate, keeping a slight bend in your knees. Fully straighten your arms so that you feel a complete stretch in your lats. Slowly pull the V-bar to your lower abdomen, keeping your elbows close to your sides and your lower back slightly arched. As the handle touches your body, squeeze your shoulder blades together, and then reverse direction, slowly returning to the start position. To perform the move at home, attach a strength band to a stationary object or secure it around your feet and perform the move as described.

At Home

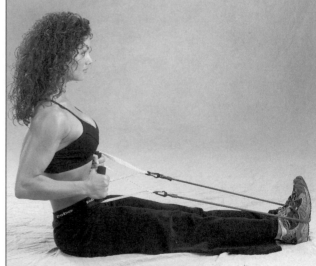

ONE-ARM SEATED ROW

This is a cool variation of the seated row. Begin by grasping a loop handle attached to a low pulley with your left hand. Sit down in front of the pulley with your feet against the footplate, keeping a slight bend in your knees. Fully straighten your arm so that you feel a complete stretch in your left lat. Slowly pull the loop handle to your lower left side, keeping your elbow in and lower back slightly arched at all times. As you reach the finish position, contract your left lat, and then reverse direction, slowly returning to the start position. Repeat with your right arm after finishing the desired number of reps with your left. To perform at home, attach a strength band to a stationary object and perform the move as described.

At Home

BACK EXERCISES

ONE-ARM DUMBBELL ROW

Because this is a unilateral movement, it allows you to focus closely on each side of your back. Begin by placing your left hand and left knee on a flat bench, planting your right foot firmly on the floor. Your torso should be parallel to the ground through the entire movement. Grasp a dumbbell in your right hand with your palm facing you and let it hang by your side. Keeping your elbow close to your body, pull the dumbbell upward and back until it touches your hip. Make sure your back remains flat and tight throughout the move. Feel a contraction in your upper back, and then reverse direction, slowly returning to the start position. Repeat with your left arm after finishing the desired number of reps with your right.

T-BAR ROW

Begin by standing with your body bent forward and your lower back arched. Hang your arms straight down from your shoulders with your palms turned toward you and grasp a T-bar. Keeping your elbows close to your sides, pull the bar up as high as possible. Contract the muscles in your upper back, and then reverse direction, slowly returning to the start position. It's extremely important to maintain a slight hyperextension of the lower back during this exercise as any spinal bend can result in severe injury.

ONE-ARM STANDING LOW ROW

Begin by grasping the loop of a low pulley with your right hand. Step back from the machine and straighten your right arm so you feel a stretch in your right lat. Keep your right leg back and bend your left leg so your weight is forward. Slowly pull the loop toward your right side, keeping your elbow close. Contract your right lat, and then reverse direction, slowly returning to the start position. Repeat with your left arm after finishing the desired number reps with your right.

STRAIGHT-ARM PULL-DOWN

Because this exercise provides continuous tension throughout the move, it's a good alternative to dumbbell pullovers. Begin by taking an overhand grip on a straight bar attached to a high pulley. Slightly bend your elbows and bring the bar to eye level. Keeping your upper body tilted forward, slowly pull the bar down in a semicircle until it touches your upper thighs. Contract your back muscles, and then reverse direction, slowly returning to the start position. To perform at home, attach a strength band to a stationary object and perform the move as described.

At Home

BACK EXERCISES

DUMBBELL PULLOVER

This is a good, basic movement for the lats and serrati. Begin by lying on a flat bench. Grasp a dumbbell with both hands and raise it directly over your face. Keeping your arms slightly bent, slowly lower the dumbbell behind your head as far as comfortably possible, feeling a complete stretch in your lats. Then reverse direction, squeezing your lats as you return to the start position.

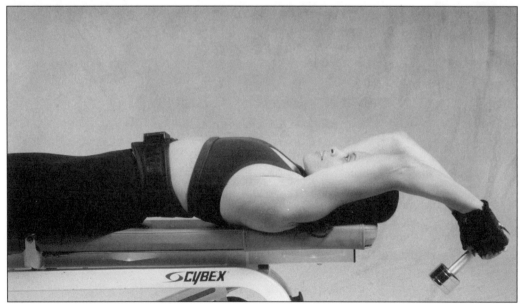

LYING CABLE PULLOVER

Begin by lying on a flat bench placed in front of a low pulley machine. Attach a rope to the low pulley unit, grasp the rope with both hands and raise it directly over your face. Keeping your arms slightly bent, pull the rope up in a semicircle until it is directly over your head. Contract your lats, and then reverse direction, slowly returning to the start position.

Shapely Shoulders

The shoulders are one of the most aesthetically pleasing muscle groups; when properly developed, they can literally redefine your physique. The importance of nicely rounded shoulders is clearly evident in the women's clothing industry. Most of today's leading fashion designers incorporate shoulder pads into their garments to accentuate the shoulder-to-waist differential. This creates the classic hourglass figure coveted by women throughout the ages.

Poorly developed shoulders cannot be concealed when you wear a strapless dress or bikini. The shoulders are prominent in a variety of fashions and affect the way clothing hangs on your body. Fortunately, through targeted bodysculpting, you can acquire a natural V taper that accentuates a shapely, curvaceous physique without artificial padding. After sculpting these muscles to perfection, it won't matter what outfit you wear—you'll look great in them all!

Bodysculpting Routine

The deltoids have three distinct heads—anterior (front), medial (middle), and posterior (rear)—whose fibers run in different directions. To develop the shoulders optimally, your routine should include at least one exercise for each head of the deltoid. Hence, exercises for the shoulders are classified by the deltoid head that they primarily stress.

• **Group 1**—overhead presses, front raises, and similar variations. These exercises target the anterior deltoid. Contrary to popular belief, overhead presses are mainly a front deltoid move. While all three deltoid heads (as well as many supporting muscles of the shoulder) are involved during performance, the anterior portion is in a position to directly oppose gravity and therefore acts as the prime mover. Front raises, on the other hand, are isolation movements that specifically target the anterior deltoid with only minimal stress to the other heads.

• **Group 2**—lateral raises, upright rows, and similar variations. These exercises emphasize the medial portion of the deltoid, which creates the coveted "cap" on your shoulders (eliminating the need for shoulder pads). This increases your shoulder-to-waist differential, which creates the illusion of a smaller waist. Lateral raises are isolation movements that allow you to train the middle deltoid to the relative exclusion of the other shoulder muscles; lateral raises are arguably the most important overall exercise for the deltoids. Upright rows, besides

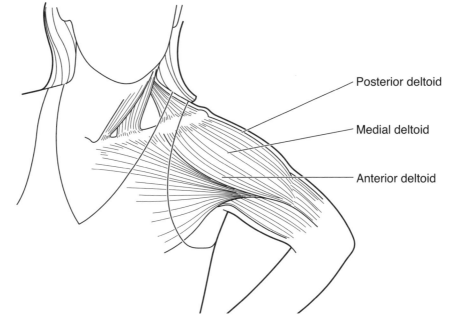

■ Muscles of the shoulders.

stressing the middle deltoid, activate supporting muscles of the upper back and shoulders. They are a good choice for adding variety to your routine.

• **Group 3**—bent lateral raises and similar variations. These movements target the posterior head of the deltoid, perhaps the most difficult shoulder muscle to develop. The rear deltoids receive little secondary stress from other exercises and therefore need direct stimulation through isolation movements. Ignoring these muscles not only throws off your symmetry but also can cause a structural imbalance among the deltoid heads, which can lead to shoulder joint injury.

Bodysculpting Tips

1. The front deltoid receives a great deal of stress in most chest movements and therefore can overshadow the other muscles of your shoulders. Consequently, use isolation movements for the front deltoid (such as the front raise) sparingly to avoid overdeveloping this muscle at the expense of the middle and rear heads.

2. The Arnold press is a little-used exercise that can add variety to your workout and improve the deltoids' overall shape. It helps to stimulate additional muscle fibers due to horizontal shoulder joint abduction neglected by other pressing movements. Used judiciously, it provides an effective complement to standard shoulder presses.

3. The shoulders' width is dictated mainly by the medial head of the deltoid. If you have a naturally blocky waist, you should really concentrate on shaping this area to its fullest extent. This has the effect of making your waist look smaller, thereby producing a more curvaceous appearance. Alternatively, if you are naturally broad shouldered or wasp-waisted, shoulder width isn't an issue, and it's best to focus on maintaining balance.

4. Shoulder injuries are common due to poor warm-up and training technique. Because the shoulder joint is highly mobile (it is the only joint that can move freely in any direction), it is more fragile and unstable than other joints. Given the high potential for damage to this area, extra care should be taken to warm up the region. Needless to say, training with proper form is an absolute must.

TABLE 8.1   EXERCISES FOR THE SHOULDERS

GROUP	EXERCISES
Group 1	Front dumbbell raise Arnold press Dumbbell shoulder press Machine shoulder press Military press Behind-the-neck press
Group 2	Dumbbell lateral raise Cable lateral raise Cable upright row Machine lateral raise Dumbbell upright row
Group 3	Bent lateral raise Cable bent lateral raise Machine rear lateral raise Bench rear lateral raise

TABLE 8.2   SAMPLE TARGETED WORKOUTS FOR THE SHOULDERS

WORKOUT	IN THE GYM		AT HOME	
	Exercise	Sets	Exercise	Sets
1	Arnold press (p. 78)	3	Dumbbell shoulder press (p. 79)	3
	Front dumbbell raise (p. 77) supersetted with machine rear lateral raise (p. 90)	2	Dumbbell upright row (p. 87)	3
	Bench rear lateral raise (p. 91)	3	Bent lateral raise (p. 88)	3
2	Dumbbell shoulder press (p. 79) supersetted with dumbbell lateral raise (p. 83)	3	Arnold press (p. 78) supersetted with dumbbell lateral raise (p. 83)	3
	Machine rear lateral raise (p. 90)	3	Bench rear lateral raise (p. 91)	3
3	Military press (p. 81) supersetted with machine lateral raise (p. 86)	3		
	Bent lateral raise (p. 88)	2		
4	Machine shoulder press (p. 80)	3		
	Cable lateral raise (p. 84)	2		
	Cable bent lateral raise (p. 89)	3		

FRONT DUMBBELL RAISE

This move is most useful if your front deltoids are underdeveloped with respect to the medial and posterior heads; if not, use it sparingly. Begin by grasping two dumbbells and allow them to hang by your hips. With a slight bend in your elbows, slowly raise the dumbbells directly in front of your body to shoulder level. Contract your deltoids, and then slowly return the weights along the same path to the start position.

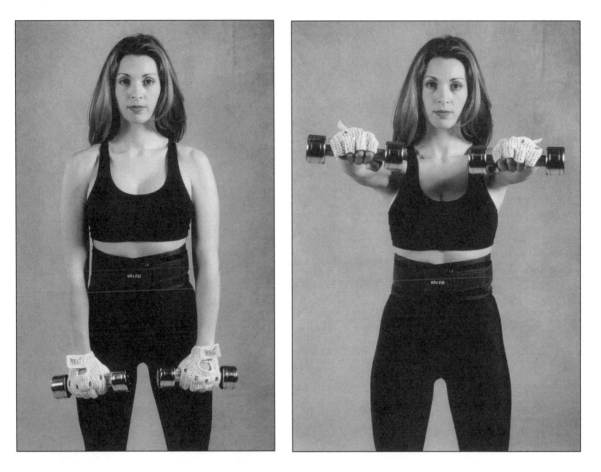

SHOULDER EXERCISES

ARNOLD PRESS

This move was named after Arnold Schwarzenegger, who considered it his favorite shoulder exercise—enough said! Begin by sitting at the edge of a flat bench. Grasp two dumbbells and bring the weights to shoulder level with your palms facing toward your body. Press the dumbbells directly upward, simultaneously rotating your hands so that your palms face forward during the last portion of the movement. Touch the weights together over your head, and then slowly return them along the same path, rotating your hands back to the start position.

DUMBBELL SHOULDER PRESS

This is the gold standard of compound shoulder exercises. Begin by sitting at the edge of a flat bench. Grasp two dumbbells and bring the weights to shoulder level with your palms facing away from your body. Slowly press the dumbbells directly upward and in, allowing them to touch together directly over your head. Contract your deltoids and then slowly return the dumbbells along the same arc back to the start position.

MACHINE SHOULDER PRESS

Begin by sitting in a shoulder press machine. Grasp the machine handles with your palms facing away from your body. Slowly press the handles directly upward and over your head, contracting your deltoids at the top of the move. Then slowly return the handles back to the start position.

MILITARY PRESS

Begin by sitting at the edge of a flat bench. Grasp a barbell and bring it to the level of your upper chest with your palms facing away from your body. Slowly press the barbell directly upward and over your head, contracting your deltoids at the top of the move. Then, slowly return the bar along the same arc back to the start position.

SHOULDER EXERCISES

BEHIND-THE-NECK PRESS

Begin by sitting at the edge of a flat bench. Grasp a bar and bring it behind your neck with your palms facing forward. Slowly press the barbell directly upward and over your head, contracting your deltoids at the top of the move. Then, slowly return the bar along the same arc back to the start position. Be careful with this move, as it can cause impingement of the shoulder. Those with existing shoulder problems should stay away from this exercise.

DUMBBELL LATERAL RAISE

This is the prototypical move for targeting the medial deltoids. Begin by grasping two dumbbells and allow them to hang by your hips. With your elbows slightly bent, raise the dumbbells up and out to the sides until they reach shoulder level. At the top of the movement, the rear of the dumbbells should be slightly higher than the front. Contract your deltoids and then slowly return the weights along the same path back to the start position.

SHOULDER EXERCISES

CABLE LATERAL RAISE

Begin by grasping a loop handle attached to a low pulley apparatus with your left hand, and stand so that your right side is facing the pulley. With a slight bend at your elbow, raise the handle across your body, up and out to the side until it reaches the level of your shoulder. Contract your deltoids at the top of the movement, and then slowly return the handle back to the start position. After completing the desired number of reps, repeat the process on your right side. The movement can also be done with both arms at the same time. To perform the exercise at home, attach a strength band to a stationary object and perform the move as described.

At Home

CABLE UPRIGHT ROW

This is my favorite variation of the upright row. Begin by taking a shoulder-width grip on a rope that is attached to a low cable pulley. Allow your arms to hang down from your shoulders and assume a comfortable stance with your knees slightly bent. Slowly pull the rope upward along the line of your body until your upper arm approaches shoulder level, keeping your elbows higher than your wrists at all times. Contract your deltoids, and then slowly lower the rope along the same path back to the start position. To perform the move at home, attach a strength band to a stationary object and perform the move as described.

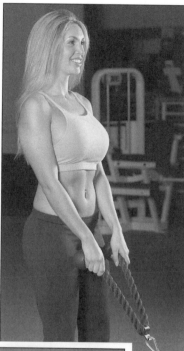

At Home

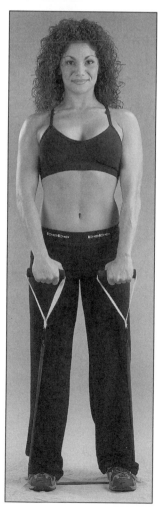

MACHINE LATERAL RAISE

Begin by sitting face forward in a lateral raise machine. With your elbows slightly bent, grasp the machine handles with your palms facing one another. Raise your arms up and out to the sides until they reach shoulder level. Contract your deltoids, and then slowly return back to the start position.

DUMBBELL UPRIGHT ROW

Begin by grasping two dumbbells and allow your arms to hang down from your shoulders with your palms facing in toward your body. Assume a comfortable stance and keep your knees slightly bent. Keeping your elbows higher than your wrists at all times, slowly raise the dumbbells upward along the line of your body until your upper arms approach shoulder level. Contract your deltoids and then slowly lower the dumbbells along the same path back to the start position.

BENT LATERAL RAISE

Begin by grasping two dumbbells and bend your torso forward so that it is almost parallel with the ground. Allow the dumbbells to hang down in front of your body. With your elbows slightly bent, raise the dumbbells up and out to the sides until your arms are parallel with the ground. Contract your deltoids at the top of the movement, and then slowly return the dumbbells back to the start position. Make sure that you don't swing your body to complete a rep as this takes stress away from the target muscles.

CABLE BENT LATERAL RAISE

Attach a loop handle to a low pulley, and grasp the handle with your right hand. Bend your torso forward so that it is almost parallel with the ground. With a slight bend of your elbow, raise the handle across your body and up and out to the side until your arm is parallel with the ground. Contract your deltoids at the top of the movement, and then slowly return the handle back to the start position. After completing the desired number of reps, repeat the process on your left side. To perform this move at home, attach a strength band to a stationary object and perform the move as described.

At Home

SHOULDER EXERCISES

MACHINE REAR LATERAL RAISE

Begin by sitting face forward in a pec deck apparatus. With your elbows slightly bent, grasp the machine handles with your palms facing one another. Slowly pull the handles back in a semicircular arc as far as comfortably possible, keeping your arms parallel with the ground at all times. Contract your rear deltoids, and then reverse direction, returning the handles back to the start position.

BENCH REAR LATERAL RAISE

I like this move because it stabilizes your body so that ancillary muscle actions are minimized. Begin by lying prone on an incline bench set at an incline of approximately 30 degrees. Grasp two dumbbells and allow them to hang down in front of your body. With your elbows slightly bent, raise the dumbbells up and out to the sides until your arms are parallel with the ground. Contract your deltoids at the top of the movement, and then slowly return the dumbbells back to the start position.

Brandy Flores

My story: Being a model and an actress I have to stay fit. But when you feel good about yourself it changes how you feel about everything in your life.

Achievements: Placed in top 5 of various competitions

©Brandy Flores

What motivated you to begin a weight-training program? How old were you when you started?

I started lifting weights when I was about 18, but I didn't get really serious about it until I was 20. I liked the look of the women I would see in fitness magazines and I was looking for another outlet for working out.

How do you feel about using nutritional supplements?

I truly believe in them. It's hard to eat 4–5 meals a day and stick to your diet without using protein drinks or protein bars.

What is your nutritional philosophy?

Eat healthy 6 days a week and don't beat yourself up over it if you break during the week—just get back it to next day. Think of eating healthy as lifestyle change, not a diet.

What other types of physical activity do you do to diversify your fitness regimen?

I started doing Pilates and I love it. I do cardio 6 days a week and Pilates twice a week. I run stairs and jog with my dog to mix it up.

How do you reward yourself after a great workout?

I don't . . . you should always try to have a good workout. It's part of life.

Do you have any training tips you'd like to pass on?

Give it a try. Start out slowly and build your way up.

www.brandyflores.com

9

Beautiful Biceps

The biceps are traditionally the most glorified of all muscles. Shapely biceps are a symbol of fitness and strength, apparent whenever you flex your arm. In combination with the triceps, they give your arms an eye-catching appearance and make you look great in any sleeveless outfit.

The biceps also are essential in carrying out many of life's daily chores. You use your biceps in almost every lifting action, whether you are picking up your kids, putting groceries in your car, or rearranging your furniture. By strengthening this muscle group, you'll be able to perform these tasks more easily, improving your overall quality of life.

Bodysculpting Routine

The biceps is a two-headed muscle that sits on the top portion of your upper arm. Most women do not store significant amounts of body fat in this area (as opposed to the triceps region, where fat is readily deposited), so they tend to notice biceps development more quickly than development in other muscles.

Because the long head of the biceps crosses the shoulder (glenohumeral) joint, it is more active during exercises where the shoulder is extended (elbows behind the body) and less active where the shoulder is flexed (elbows in front of the body). What's more, varying the grip used influences muscular stress to the area: exercises that employ a supinated grip (palms facing toward your body maximize stress to the biceps, while exercises that use a neutral grip (palms facing each other) shift the emphasis away from the biceps and allow the brachialis to take over a majority of the work. Accordingly, exercises for the biceps are classified both by whether stretch is applied to the long head and by the grip used in performance.

- **Group 1**—incline curls, seated curls, EZ curls, and similar variations. These movements target the long head of the biceps (which sits on the outer portion of your upper arm) by increasing the stretch of the muscle. As a rule, the more your elbows are pulled behind your body, the greater the stress to the long head (that is, incline curls target the long head more than seated curls). Developing the long head adds height to the biceps and makes your arms really stand out when viewed from the side.

BULKING UP

Weight training can sculpt the body many different ways. You can structure a weight-training routine to add mass, increase strength, improve muscular tone, or change your body in many other ways. Contrary to popular opinion, most women find it extremely difficult to add a significant amount of muscle. (Many men have the same difficulty.) Nearly all women do not have the capacity to become extremely muscular, primarily due to low testosterone levels.

Moreover, although it can take years to develop a muscular physique, it is relatively easy to reduce muscle mass. Simply taking time off from training or reducing intensity will result in muscular atrophy. Hence, worrying that you will get too big or muscular from training should be the least of your concerns.

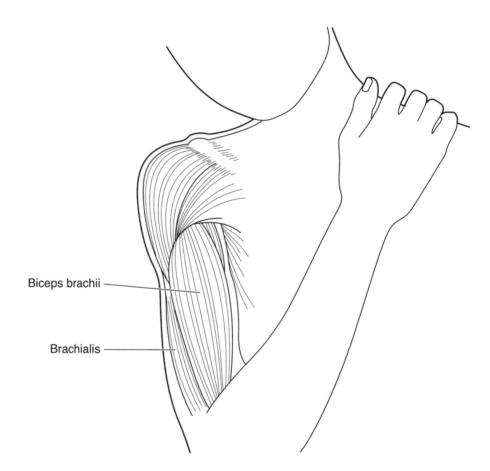

Biceps brachii

Brachialis

■ Muscles of the biceps.

• **Group 2**—preacher curls, concentration curls, prone incline curls, and similar variations. These movements limit the stretch of the long head, thereby emphasizing the short head to a greater extent. This area of the biceps is on the inner portion of your upper arm and helps to give the muscle a full, rounded appearance.

• **Group 3**—hammer curls and similar variations. These movements use a neutral grip (palms facing one another) and therefore target the brachialis, a complementary muscle of the biceps that is involved in elbow flexion. The brachialis sits between your biceps and triceps and helps give detail to your upper arm. Moreover, when properly developed, it helps to delineate the contour of your biceps and triceps, producing a well-defined line between the two.

Bodysculpting Tips

1. For a different feel, you can perform curls with a pronated grip (palms facing away from your body). This shifts emphasis much more to the forearm muscles. But unless you really need extra forearm work, use this grip sparingly, mostly for variety.

2. It is often beneficial to use an EZ-curl bar, rather than a straight bar, when performing barbell exercises. The EZ-curl bar is curved to allow a natural tilt of the wrist. This can help alleviate pressure on the wrist joint—a common weak spot for women—making curling exercises more comfortable to execute.

3. The biceps are active in exercises for the back, receiving secondary stress in virtually all back-related movements. Moreover, they are a relatively small muscle complex, requiring limited training volume for maximal stimulation. Hence, you must use caution in working these muscles to avoid overtraining. If you find that your biceps are not responding the way you would like, reduce the overall training volume, frequency, or both to allow more time for recuperation.

4. Genes determine the length of your biceps. If you have a short biceps muscle and a long biceps tendon, there is little you can do to lengthen the muscle (sorry, but that's the way it is). By adequately developing this area, however, you can offset a short biceps muscle by creating the illusion of fullness in the region where the muscle tapers off.

TABLE 9.1   EXERCISES FOR THE BICEPS

GROUP	EXERCISES
Group 1	Standing EZ curl
	21s with EZ-curl bar
	Seated dumbbell curl
	Cable curl
	Incline curl
Group 2	Preacher curl
	One-arm dumbbell preacher curl
	Concentration curl
	Prone incline curl
Group 3	Hammer curl
	Cable-rope hammer curl
	Machine hammer curl
	Incline hammer curl

TABLE 9.2 SAMPLE TARGETED WORKOUTS FOR THE BICEPS

WORKOUT	IN THE GYM		AT HOME	
	Exercise	**Sets**	**Exercise**	**Sets**
1	Incline curl (p. 101)	3	Incline curl (p. 101) supersetted with prone incline curl (p. 105)	3
	One-arm dumbbell preacher curl (p. 103)	3	Cable-rope hammer curl (p. 107)	2
	Hammer curl (p. 106)	2		
2	Cable curl (p. 100) supersetted with prone incline curl (p. 105)	2	Seated dumbbell curl (p. 99)	3
	Incline hammer curl (p. 109)	3	Preacher curl (p. 102)	2
			Hammer curl (p. 106)	2
3	Seated dumbbell curl (p. 99) supersetted with preacher curl (p. 102) and cable-rope hammer curl (p. 107)	2		
4	Standing EZ curl (p. 97)	3		
	Prone incline curl (p. 105)	2		
	Machine hammer curl (p. 108)	2		

STANDING EZ CURL

I prefer this movement to the straight-bar curl because it alleviates pressure on the wrists. Begin by grasping an EZ-curl bar with a palms-up, shoulder-width grip. Maintain a slight bend of your knees and press your elbows into your sides, keeping them stable throughout the move. Slowly curl the bar up toward your shoulders, and contract your biceps at the top of the move. Then slowly reverse direction and return to the start position.

BICEPS EXERCISES

21S WITH EZ-CURL BAR

This is a cool variation of the standard curl that allows you to improve strength at your weak point in the move. Begin by grasping an EZ-curl bar with your hands shoulder-width apart and your palms facing up. Slightly bend your knees and press your elbows to your sides, keeping them stable through the move. Slowly curl the bar until your elbows are at a 90-degree angle. Return to the start position. After performing seven reps, curl the bar to a 90-degree angle, then slowly curl the weight to your shoulders. Perform seven reps of curls to your shoulders, returning only to the 90-degree start position. Finally, lower the bar fully and perform seven complete reps, bringing the weight to shoulder level and returning to a fully-stretched position.

SEATED DUMBBELL CURL

This is a good, basic biceps developer. Begin by sitting at the edge of a flat bench. Grasp a pair of dumbbells and allow them to hang at your sides with your palms facing forward. Press your elbows into your sides and keep them stable throughout the move. Slowly curl the dumbbells up toward your shoulders, and contract your biceps at the top of the move. Then slowly reverse direction and return to the start position.

BICEPS EXERCISES

CABLE CURL

This is one of my favorite biceps exercises. Begin by grasping a straight bar attached to a low pulley. Using a palms-up, shoulder-width grip, slightly bend your knees and press your elbows to your sides, stabilizing them through the move. Slowly curl the bar toward your shoulders, and contract your biceps at the top of the move. Return to the start position.

INCLINE CURL

This exercise really targets the long head of the biceps. Begin by lying back on a 45-degree incline bench. Grasp two dumbbells and allow the weights to hang by your hips with your palms facing forward. Keeping your upper arm stable, slowly curl the dumbbells upward toward your shoulders. Make sure your elbows stay back throughout the movement. Contract your biceps, and then slowly return the weights back to the start position.

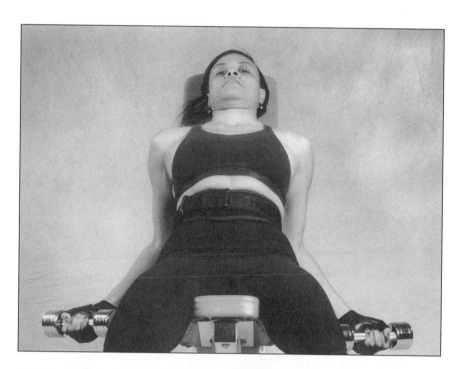

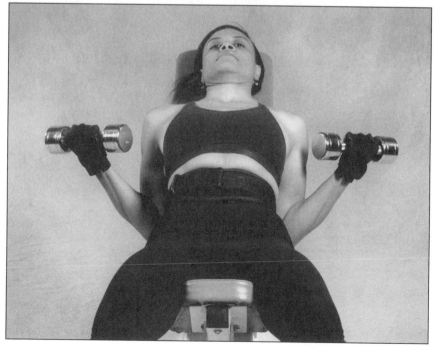

BICEPS EXERCISES

PREACHER CURL

Begin by grasping an EZ-curl bar and placing your upper arms on top of the pad of a preacher bench. Keeping your upper arms stationary, slowly curl the bar toward your shoulders. Contract your biceps at the top of the move. Reverse direction, returning to the start position.

ONE-ARM DUMBBELL PREACHER CURL

Begin by grasping a dumbbell with your right hand. Place the upper portion of your right arm on an incline bench and allow your right forearm to extend just short of locking the elbow. Keeping your upper arm pressed to the bench, slowly curl the dumbbell upward toward your shoulder. Contract your biceps, and then slowly return the weight back to the start position. After completing the desired number of reps, repeat the process with your left arm.

CONCENTRATION CURL

Begin by sitting at the edge of a flat bench with your legs wide apart. Grasp a dumbbell in your right hand and brace your right triceps on the inside of your right knee. Straighten your right arm so that it hangs down near the floor. Slowly curl the weight up and in along the line of your body, contracting your biceps at the top of the move. Then, slowly reverse direction and return to the start position. After completing the desired number of reps, repeat the process with your left arm.

PRONE INCLINE CURL

This unique move is one of the best for targeting the short head of the biceps. Begin by lying face down on a 45-degree incline bench. Grasp two dumbbells and allow the weights to hang straight down from your shoulders with your palms facing forward. Slowly curl the dumbbells upward toward your shoulders, keeping your upper arms stable throughout the movement. Contract your biceps, and then slowly return the weights back to the start position.

BICEPS EXERCISES

HAMMER CURL

This is a terrific move for targeting the brachialis. Begin by grasping a pair of dumbbells and allowing them to hang at your sides with your palms facing each other. Assume a comfortable seat with a slight bend in your knees, and press your elbows to your sides, keeping them stable throughout the move. Slowly curl the dumbbells up toward your shoulders, and contract your biceps at the top of the move. Then slowly reverse direction and return to the start position.

CABLE-ROPE HAMMER CURL

Begin by grasping both ends of a rope that is attached to a low cable pulley. Bring your arms to your sides with your palms facing each other. Assume a comfortable stance with a slight bend in your knees, and press your elbows to your sides, keeping them stable throughout the move. Slowly curl the rope up toward your shoulders, and contract your biceps at the top of the move. Then slowly reverse direction and return to the start position. To perform the move at home, attach a strength band to a stationary object or under your feet and perform the move as described.

At Home

MACHINE HAMMER CURL

Hammer curl machines are somewhat rare, but if your gym has one, use it. It provides a nice alternative to other variations of the hammer curl. Begin by sitting in a hammer curl machine and grasping the handles of the unit. Place your elbows on the pads with your palms facing each other. Slowly curl the handles up toward your shoulders, and contract your biceps at the top of the move. Then slowly reverse direction and return to the start position.

INCLINE HAMMER CURL

Begin by lying back on a 45-degree incline bench. Grasp two dumbbells and allow the weights to hang by your hips with your palms facing each other. Keeping your upper arms stable, slowly curl the dumbbells upward toward your shoulders. Make sure your elbows stay back throughout the movement. Contract your biceps, and then slowly return the weights back to the start position.

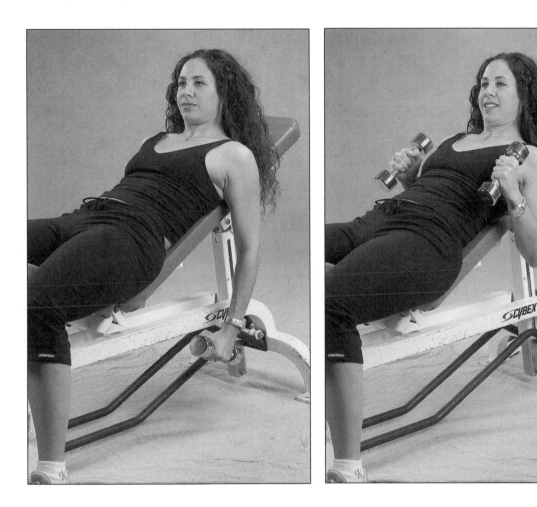

Linda Cusmano

My story: I had become anorexic after my father passed away when I was 17 years old. By my early 20s I was very unhealthy, although recovered [from anorexia]. I had atrophied my muscle and noticed I needed to improve my physique. That's when I began weight training. I gained muscle very easily, which coaxed me to become a fitness competitor.

Achievements: 2nd Place Fitness Winner Western Canadian ANBC, 4th Place Winner Short Class Bodybuilding, 21st Place in 2000 Fitness Universe Pageant

©Sarah Murray

What do you consider your best fitness accomplishment?

I am proud to have gained the Pro Canadian Fitness Champion title. I am a chronic bronchial asthmatic and fitness helps me to keep healthy.

How do you feel about using nutritional supplements?

I believe that you can achieve fitness goals with a healthy diet but at a competitive level it is realistic to use supplementation to better your health and gains.

What is your nutritional philosophy? Do you have a "power" food?

I stick mainly to a vegetarian diet although I do eat fish and occasionally dairy. I find vegetarian curries made from beans are a great power food, but sushi will always win hands down for being the lightest power food you can find.

What other types of physical activity do you do to diversify your fitness regimen?

Kickboxing, basic gymnastics, plyometrics, in-line skating, dance.

How do you reward yourself after a great workout?

A nice shot of juice with creatine! The great workout is reward enough!

Do you have any training tips you'd like to pass on?

Don't be afraid to squat, especially if you want to firm and shape your butt. Don't be afraid to train hard and build muscle. Women will not get bulky by weight training so don't avoid weights. Lastly, don't think that cardio or thermogenics are your only way to getting lean.

www.lindacusmano.com

10

Toned Triceps

Poorly developed triceps muscles are an obvious sign of aging. Because a woman's body tends to store fat in this area, the triceps are one of the biggest problem spots on the female physique. When left untrained, your triceps atrophy, and you eventually develop "bat wings"—loose, flabby, hanging skin. This not a pretty sight for those who want to look fit. Furthermore, the triceps are heavily involved in many exercises for your chest and shoulders. When your triceps are weak, performing these movements can be difficult or impossible. This reduces your training capacity and, ultimately, your ability to redefine your body.

Fortunately, the triceps respond rapidly to training. Once you reduce body fat to acceptable levels, targeted bodysculpting gives the back of your arms a taut, toned appearance. In short order, you'll want to go sleeveless year round!

Bodysculpting Routine

The triceps is a three-headed muscle that resides on the bottom and middle portions of your upper arm, constituting roughly two thirds of the mass in this area. Although total isolation of the individual heads of the triceps is not possible, you can shift the emphasis to different aspects of the muscle by varying the stretch at the shoulder joint. Therefore, exercises for the triceps are classified into three basic positions that shift stress to the various heads.

- **Group 1**—overhead extensions and similar variations. When you extend your upper arm overhead in the fully-stretched position, the long head of your triceps is maximally involved. This is the part of the triceps that sits on the bottom of your upper arm, the place that many women complain is flabby. (If your arms jiggle in the wind, you need to develop this area!) Overhead exercises for the triceps are the best way to counteract sagging arms.

- **Group 2**—kickbacks, press-downs, dips, and similar variations. When your upper arm is kept close to your body, you substantially reduce the stretch of the long head of your triceps. Thus, the medial and lateral heads of your triceps (the part of the triceps on the upper arm's middle portion that forms a "tail") receive a greater degree of muscular stimulation. Toning this area adds detail and hardness to the upper arm—an indication of superb feminine conditioning.

111

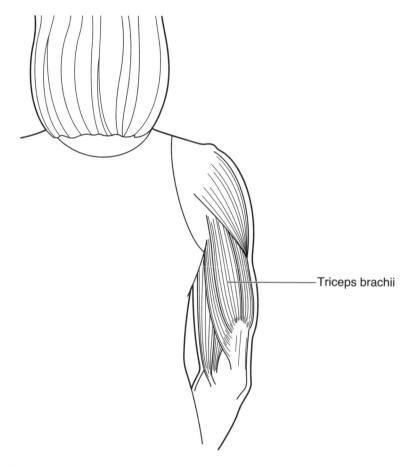

Triceps brachii

■ Muscles of the triceps.

• **Group 3**—nosebreakers, lying triceps extensions, and similar variations. By placing the upper arm at a 90-degree angle to the torso, these movements stress all three heads of the triceps in roughly equal fashion. They are excellent overall triceps builders and really help to promote optimal development. Make sure that your elbows don't move during performance, though; there is a natural tendency to extend your shoulder as you straighten your arm, which removes stress from the target muscles.

Bodysculpting Tips

1. As previously stated, the triceps receive secondary stimulation in many shoulder and chest exercises (and even some back exercises, too). They are strongly involved in all presses, as well as other pushing movements. Thus, like the biceps, they are highly susceptible to overtraining. Although the triceps are a larger muscle complex than the biceps and thus can tolerate a slightly greater volume of training, you should still be sensitive to the amount of work that you give this area. As a rule, keep the total number of sets to no more than nine per session.

2. Using a rope for triceps press-downs can help target the lateral head of the muscle. Although the long and medial heads of your triceps receive secondary stress from many pressing exercises for the chest and shoulders, the lateral head

receives less stimulation. Rope press-downs use a wrist position that increases stress to the lateral head, helping to bring out greater detail in the middle portion of your upper arm. You can apply further stress to this area by turning your wrists at the end of the movement (so the backs of your hands face one another on the contraction). This subtle turn of the wrist activates additional muscle fibers neglected in other triceps movements.

3. You should keep your elbows close to your body in all exercises for the triceps. This prevents your shoulders and chest from taking over the performance of the movement. Moreover, because the main purpose of the triceps is to extend the elbow, you should keep your upper arm stable throughout each repetition. Isolation is the key to shaping the triceps. Attention to these two factors is essential for peak results.

TABLE 10.1   EXERCISES FOR THE TRICEPS

GROUP	EXERCISES
Group 1	Two-arm overhead dumbbell extension
	Machine overhead extension
	One-arm overhead dumbbell extension
	Two-arm overhead cable extension
	Overhead rope extension
Group 2	Triceps press-down
	One-arm reverse press-down
	Close-grip bench press
	Dumbbell kickback
	Cable kickback
	Triceps dip
	Cross-bench dip
	Triceps machine dip
Group 3	Nosebreaker
	One-arm lying dumbbell triceps extension
	Two-arm lying dumbbell triceps extension
	Lying cable triceps extension

TABLE 10.2   SAMPLE TARGETED WORKOUTS FOR THE TRICEPS

WORKOUT	IN THE GYM		AT HOME	
	Exercise	**Sets**	**Exercise**	**Sets**
1	Two-arm overhead dumbbell extension (p. 115) supersetted with triceps pressdown (p. 120)	2	Two-arm overhead dumbbell extension (p. 115)	3
	One-arm overhead dumbbell extension (p. 117)	3	Dumbbell kickback (p. 123)	3
	One-arm lying dumbbell triceps extension (p. 129)	2	One-arm lying dumbbell triceps extension (p. 129)	2
2	One-arm overhead dumbbell extension (p. 117)	3	Overhead rope extension (p. 119)	3
	Triceps dip (p. 125) supersetted with nosebreaker (p. 128)	2	Triceps dip (p. 125) supersetted with two-arm lying dumbbell triceps extension (p. 130)	2
3	Machine overhead extension (p. 116)	3		
	One-arm reverse press-down (p. 121)	3		
	Two-arm lying dumbbell triceps extension (p. 130)	2		
4	Overhead rope extension (p. 119)	2		
	Triceps machine dip (p. 127)	2		
	Lying cable triceps extension (p. 131)	3		

TWO-ARM OVERHEAD DUMBBELL EXTENSION

Begin by grasping the stem of a dumbbell with both hands. Raise your arms overhead, bend your elbows, and allow the weight to hang down behind your head as far as comfortably possible. Slowly straighten your arms, keeping your elbows back and pointed toward the ceiling throughout the move. Contract your triceps, and then slowly lower the weight along the same path back to the start position.

MACHINE OVERHEAD EXTENSION

Begin by sitting in an overhead triceps machine. Grasp the bar with your palms turned away from you. Bend your elbows and hang your hands behind your head as far as comfortably possible. Slowly straighten your arms, keeping your elbows back and pointed to the ceiling throughout the move. Contract your triceps. Return to the start position.

ONE-ARM OVERHEAD DUMBBELL EXTENSION

This variation of the overhead extension can be a little easier on the elbow, than the two-arm version. Begin by grasping a dumbbell overhead in your right hand with your feet firmly planted on the floor. Bend your elbow and allow the weight to hang down behind your head as far as comfortably possible. Slowly straighten your arm, keeping your elbow back and pointed toward the ceiling throughout the move. Contract your triceps, and then slowly lower the weight along the same path back to the start position. After you have performed the desired number of reps, repeat the process with your left arm.

TRICEPS EXERCISES

TWO-ARM OVERHEAD CABLE EXTENSION

Begin by turning your body away from a low cable pulley apparatus. Bend your torso forward and grasp a straight bar attached to the pulley apparatus with your palms facing away from you. Keeping your elbows at your ears, bend your elbows and allow your hands to hang down behind your head as far as comfortably possible. Slowly straighten your arms, keeping your elbows back throughout the move. Contract your triceps, and then slowly lower the bar along the same path back to the start position.

OVERHEAD ROPE EXTENSION

Turn away from a high cable pulley. Bend forward and, with your palms facing each other, grasp the ropes attached to the pulley. Keeping your elbows at your ears, bend your elbows and hang your hands behind your head as far as comfortably possible. Slowly straighten your arms, keeping your elbows back. Contract your triceps. Return to the start position. To perform the move at home, attach a strength band under your feet and perform the move as described.

At Home

TRICEPS EXERCISES

TRICEPS PRESS-DOWN

This is a good, basic triceps move. Begin by grasping a straight bar that is attached to a high pulley apparatus with an overhand grip. Assume a shoulder-width stance, with your knees slightly bent and your torso angled slightly forward. Bend your arms so that your elbows form a 90-degree angle, keeping your elbows in at your sides. Slowly straighten your arms. Contract your triceps, and then reverse direction to return to the start position.

ONE-ARM REVERSE PRESS-DOWN

Begin by grasping with your right hand, palm facing up, a loop handle that is attached to a high pulley apparatus. Assume a shoulder-width stance, with your knees slightly bent and your torso angled slightly forward. Bend your arm so that your elbow forms a 90-degree angle, keeping your elbow in at your side. Slowly straighten your right arm. Contract your triceps, and then reverse direction to return to the start position. After performing the desired number of repetitions, repeat the exercise with your left arm. To perform the move at home, attach a strength band to a stationary object and perform the move as described.

At Home

TRICEPS EXERCISES

CLOSE-GRIP BENCH PRESS

Begin by lying on a flat bench with your feet planted firmly on the floor. Grasp an EZ-curl bar with your hands approximately six to eight inches apart. Bring the bar directly under your pecs. Keeping your elbows close to your sides, slowly press the weight straight up, contracting your triceps. Return to the start position.

DUMBBELL KICKBACK

The dumbbell kickback is one of the best moves for targeting the medial and lateral triceps heads. Begin by leaning with your body bent forward over a bench for support so that it is nearly parallel with the ground. Grasp a dumbbell with your right hand and press your right upper arm against your side with your elbow bent at a 90-degree angle. With your palm facing your body, raise the weight by straightening your arm until it is parallel with the floor. Then reverse direction and return the weight back to the start position. After finishing the desired number of repetitions, repeat the exercise with your left arm.

CABLE KICKBACK

The cable kickback is my favorite variation of the triceps kickback. Begin by standing in front of a low cable pulley apparatus with your body bent forward so that it is nearly parallel with the ground. With your right hand, grasp a loop handle attached to a low pulley, and press your right upper arm against your side with your elbow bent at a 90-degree angle. With your palm facing your body, raise the handle by straightening your arm until it is parallel with the floor. Reverse direction and return to the start position. After finishing the desired number of repetitions, repeat the exercise with your left arm.

TRICEPS DIP

Because body weight is involved, the triceps dip can be a difficult move for many women in the initial stages of training. Over time, however, you'll readily gain the strength needed for exercise performance. Begin by placing your heels on the floor and your hands on the edge of a flat bench, keeping your arms straight. Slowly bend your elbows as far as comfortably possible, allowing your butt to descend below the level of the bench. Make sure your elbows stay close to your body throughout the move. Then reverse direction and straighten your arms, returning to the start position.

TRICEPS EXERCISES

CROSS-BENCH DIP

Place two flat benches roughly three feet apart. Place your heels on one flat bench and your hands on the edge of the other, keeping your arms straight. Slowly bend your elbows as far as comfortably possible, allowing your butt to descend below the level of the benches. Keep your elbows close to your body throughout the move. Reverse direction and straighten your arms, returning to the start position.

TRICEPS MACHINE DIP

Sit in a triceps dip machine and fasten the seat belt. Grasp the handles with your palms facing each other. Keeping your elbows at your sides, slowly press the handles down until your arms are straight. Contract your triceps. Reverse direction, returning to the start position.

TRICEPS EXERCISES

NOSEBREAKER

Don't let the name scare you; provided that you perform the movement in a controlled fashion, this is a very safe exercise. Begin by lying back on a flat bench with your feet planted firmly on the floor. Grasp an EZ-curl bar with your palms facing away from your body and straighten your arms so that the bar is directly over your chest (your arms should be perpendicular to your body). Keeping your elbows in and pointed toward the ceiling, slowly lower the bar until the weights are just above the level of your forehead. Press the bar back up until it reaches the start position.

ONE-ARM LYING DUMBBELL TRICEPS EXTENSION

Begin by lying back on a flat bench with your feet planted firmly on the floor. Grasp a dumbbell with your left hand, and straighten your arm so that the dumbbell is directly over your chest (your left arm should be perpendicular to your body). Keeping your left elbow in and pointed toward the ceiling, slowly lower the dumbbell until it reaches a point just above the level of your forehead. Press the dumbbell back up until it reaches the start position. After performing the desired number of repetitions, repeat the exercise with your right arm.

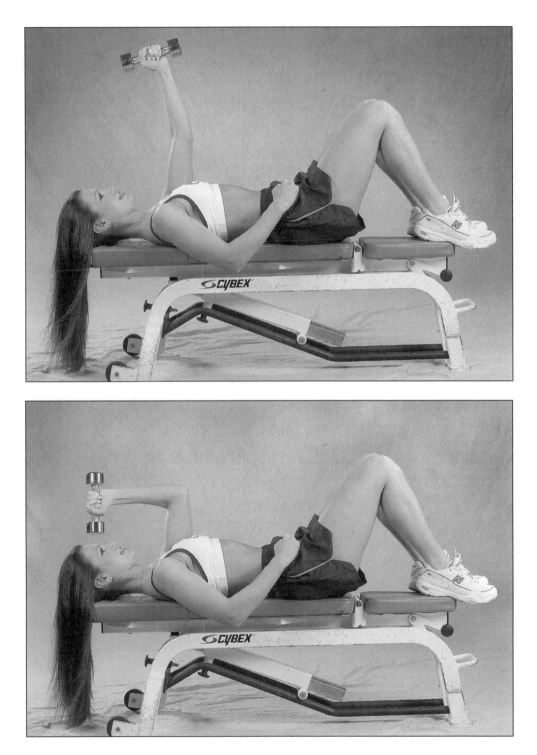

TRICEPS EXERCISES

TWO-ARM LYING DUMBBELL TRICEPS EXTENSION

Begin by lying back on a flat bench with your feet planted firmly on the floor. Grasp a dumbbell in each hand, and straighten your arms so that the dumbbells are directly over your chest (your arms should be perpendicular to your body). Keeping your elbows in and pointed toward the ceiling, slowly lower the dumbbells until they reach a point just above the level of your forehead. Press the dumbbells back up until they reach the start position.

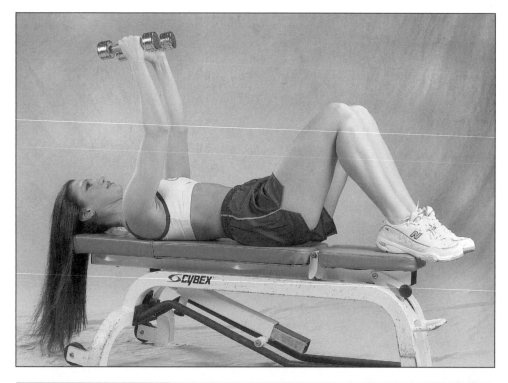

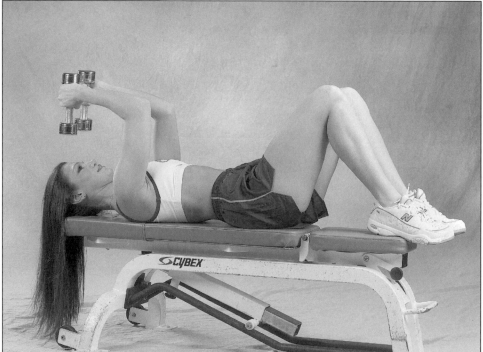

LYING CABLE TRICEPS EXTENSION

Begin by lying on a flat bench placed in front of a low pulley machine. Attach a rope to the low pulley unit and, after grasping the rope with both hands, straighten your arms so that they are perpendicular to your body. Keeping your elbows in and pointed toward the ceiling, slowly lower the rope until it reaches just above the level of your forehead. Press the rope back up until it reaches the start position.

Defined Quads

Shapely thighs define the female physique. No other body part attracts more attention from the opposite sex. A great pair of legs radiates femininity and allows you to wear the shortest of skirts with complete confidence.

Regrettably, many women are hesitant to train their thighs with sufficient intensity. Intense training, they reason, will make their lower bodies thick and bulky. By following this protocol, however, your legs not only will achieve a beautiful shape but will also appear leaner. Due to the metabolic effects of strength training, you'll help to strip away excess body fat and reveal a set of tight, toned thighs.

Bodysculpting Routine

The majority of the frontal thigh is made up of the quadriceps muscles. As the name implies, the quadriceps is composed of four distinct muscles (the rectus femoris, vastus medialis, vastus lateralis, and vastus intermedius). The three vastus muscles tend to function as one unit and therefore cannot be individually isolated during training. However, using a variety of exercises will help to maximize stimulation to all regions of the quads. What's more, the inner-thigh region (adductor muscles) can be specifically targeted with movements that bring the thigh across the midline of the body (adduction exercises). Consequently, exercises for the quadriceps are classified into compound movements, isolation movements, and direct inner thigh exercises.

- **Group 1**—squats, leg presses, lunges, and similar variations. These compound movements place direct stress on the quadriceps and secondary emphasis on the hamstrings and stabilizer muscles of the legs. Each of these exercises has unique qualities that stimulate a wide array of muscle fibers. Moreover, each movement has variations that allow additional variety.

- **Group 2**—leg extensions, front kicks, sissy squats, and similar variations. These are isolation movements that primarily work the quadriceps muscles without having a significant effect on the other thigh musculature. Because of their single-joint orientation, these exercises aren't as physically demanding as the compound movements. However, the localized burn is intense, so make sure you're prepared to deal with the temporary discomfort.

FORM

The High-Energy Fitness system mandates that you use strict form during exercise performance. This guarantees that you directly stress the target muscles, minimizing the involvement of ancillary muscles. If you lift a weight improperly, alternative muscles take stimulation away from the muscle you intend to work. Repeated use of poor form can result in disproportionate development. Worse, connective tissue (tendons and ligaments) can be unduly stressed. This is counterproductive to achieving ideal muscle tone and increases the possibility of injury.

Furthermore, "cheat" repetitions are not advised. A cheat repetition uses supporting muscles for assistance, allowing you to finish a repetition that would ordinarily be impossible. By using supporting muscles, you are cheating to complete the lift. This technique is beneficial mainly for adding mass and increasing strength. Consequently, although cheat repetitions have some benefit in a bodybuilding or powerlifting context, they have no place in bodysculpting.

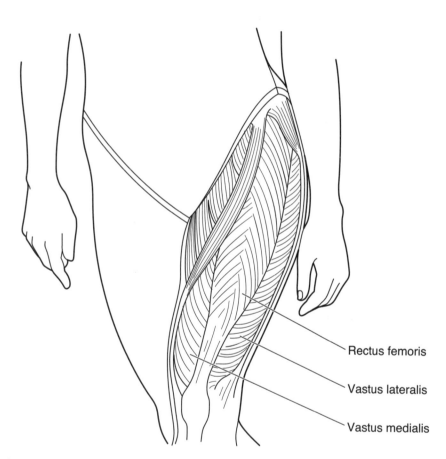

Rectus femoris

Vastus lateralis

Vastus medialis

■ Muscles of the quadriceps.

• **Group 3**—side lunges, lying adductions, cable adductions, and similar variations. These exercises target the inner thighs, one of the biggest female problem areas. Realize, though, that they only help to develop the inner thigh muscles, not strip away flab from the region. (Remember, you can't spot-reduce!) Only through a combination of proper nutrition and dedicated total-body exercise will thigh fat disappear, revealing the lean, hard muscle that you've worked so hard to develop.

Bodysculpting Tips

1.   The vastus muscles of the quadriceps are most active in exercises that involve bending the knee. It is common for women to have fat deposits around the knee, giving an undesirable shape and reducing hardness. Adding muscle tone to the vastus medialis (the "teardrop" muscle) can delineate this area, thereby accentuating your proportions. Exercises such as leg extensions are terrific for targeting the vastus muscles and maximizing lower-thigh shape.

2.   The rectus femoris (which delineates the upper portion of the thigh) is more active in movements where the hip is flexed while keeping the knee straight (or vice versa). The front kick is one of the few movements to exclude the knee joint in exercise performance, thereby stressing the rectus femoris in relative isolation from the other quadriceps muscles. Alternatively, you can stress the rectus femoris during knee extension movements by keeping the hips straight. The sissy squat is an excellent movement that employs this technique.

3.   In an effort to work various aspects of the frontal thigh, many people turn the feet in or out during exercise performance. However, the benefits of this practice are subtle, at best. Certainly, you should avoid exaggerating these foot positions, as they can cause damage to the knee, especially during *closed-chain* movements where the feet are immobile (such as the squat and leg press). When performing closed-chain movements, keep your feet turned slightly outward. Doing so allows the patella (kneecap) to move in its natural plane, maintaining the integrity of the joint. If you choose to experiment with different foot positions, do so only in *open-chain* movements, where the feet are typically free to move (such as the leg extension) and make sure to stay in a comfortable range.

4.   Make sure that you do not lock your knees on any quadriceps movement. Locking your knees reduces stimulation to the target muscles and, more important, places undue stress on the knee joint. The ligaments in this area are weak (especially the anterior cruciate ligament) and easily torn by the forces applied from locking the knee.

TABLE 11.1   EXERCISES FOR THE QUADS

GROUP	EXERCISES
Group 1	Leg press
	Squat
	Front squat
	Hack squat
	Lunge
	Walking lunge
	Jump squat
Group 2	Leg extension
	One-leg extension
	Front kick
	Sissy squat
Group 3	Side lunge
	Machine adduction
	Lying adduction
	Adductor cable pull

TABLE 11.2 SAMPLE TARGETED WORKOUTS FOR THE QUADS

WORKOUT	IN THE GYM		AT HOME	
	Exercise	**Sets**	**Exercise**	**Sets**
1	Squat (p. 137) supersetted with leg extension (p. 143)	3	Squat (p. 137) supersetted with sissy squat (p. 146)	3
	Lying adduction (p. 149)		Side lunge (p. 147)	3
2	Leg press (p. 136) supersetted with walking lunge (p. 141)	3	Lunge (p. 140)	3
	One-leg extension (p. 144)	2	Front cable kick (p. 141)	2
	Machine adduction (p. 148)	3	Lying adduction (p. 149)	3
3	Hack squat (p. 139) supersetted with jump squat (p. 142)	3		
	Front kick (p. 145)	2		
	Side lunge (p. 147)	3		
4	Front squat (p. 138)	2		
	Lunge (p. 140)	2		
	Sissy squat (p. 146)	3		
	Adductor cable pull (p. 150)	3		

QUADRICEPS EXERCISES

LEG PRESS

Begin by sitting in a leg press machine, keeping your back pressed firmly into the padded seat. Place your feet on the footplate in a shoulder-width stance. Straighten your legs and unlock the carriage release bars located on the sides of the machine. Slowly lower the weight, bringing your knees into your chest. Without bouncing at the bottom, press the weight up in a controlled fashion, stopping just short of locking out your knees. Contract your quads. Return to the start position.

SQUAT

This is the granddaddy of all quad exercises. Assume a shoulder-width stance, and rest a straight bar high on the back of your neck, grasping the bar with both hands. Slowly lower your body until your thighs are parallel with the ground. Your lower back should be slightly arched, and your heels should stay in contact with the floor at all times. When you reach a "seated" position, reverse direction by straightening your legs, and return to the start position. To do the move at home use two dumbbells and perform the exercise as described.

At Home

QUADRICEPS EXERCISES

FRONT SQUAT

This is a great movement for targeting the frontal thighs while minimizing activation of the glutes. Begin by resting a straight bar across your upper chest, holding it in place with both hands. Assuming a shoulder-width stance, slowly lower your body until your thighs are parallel with the ground. Your lower back should be slightly arched, and your heels should stay in contact with the floor at all times. When you reach a "seated" position, reverse direction by straightening your legs, and return to the start position.

HACK SQUAT

Begin by standing in a hack squat machine with the upper pads on your shoulders. Place your feet shoulder-width apart and slightly in front of you. Unlock the carriage release bars and slowly lower your body until your thighs are at an approximately 90-degree angle, keeping your heels down at all times. When you reach a "seated" position, reverse direction by straightening your legs, and return to the start position. A word of caution: this exercise stresses the knee joint and thus is contraindicated for anyone with existing knee problems.

LUNGE

For optimal intensity, perform this exercise as a "split squat." Begin by grasping two dumbbells and allow them to hang down by your sides. Take a long stride forward with your left leg, and raise your right heel so that your right foot is on its toes. Keeping your shoulders back and chin up, slowly lower your body by flexing your left knee and hip, continuing your descent until your right knee is almost in contact with floor. Reverse direction by forcibly extending the right hip and knee until you return to the start position. After performing the desired number of reps, repeat the exercise with your right foot in front.

WALKING LUNGE

This is a great alternative to the standard lunge and can really take your breath away when performed intensely. Stand in an open area with your feet shoulder-width apart. Take a long stride forward with your right leg, bringing your left knee to just above floor level. Keep your shoulders back and your head up through the move. Step forward with your left leg, bringing your right knee toward the ground. Alternate legs for the desired number of repetitions.

QUADRICEPS EXERCISES

JUMP SQUAT

This is a good movement for "shocking" your thigh muscles into better development. Begin by standing with your feet shoulder-width apart. Keeping your torso erect, slowly bend your knees, sinking into a "seated" position. When your thighs are parallel with the ground, jump into the air as high as possible. Land upright, slightly bending your knees to absorb the shock.

LEG EXTENSION

Begin by sitting back in a leg extension machine. Bend your knees and place your insteps underneath the roller pad located at the bottom of the machine. Grasp the machine's handles for support. Slowly bring your feet upward until your legs are just short of parallel with the ground. Contract your quads, and then reverse direction, returning to the start position.

QUADRICEPS EXERCISES

ONE-LEG EXTENSION

Follow the directions for leg extensions, except work just your left leg first. Repeat with your right leg after finishing the desired number of reps with your left leg.

FRONT KICK

This is a good movement for targeting the rectus femoris and thus sculpting the upper aspect of the thigh. Begin by attaching a cuff to a low cable pulley and then securing the cuff to your right ankle. Position yourself so that your body faces away from the apparatus, and grasp a sturdy portion of the machine for support. Slowly bring your foot forward and up as high as possible, contracting your right quad at the top of the movement. Then reverse direction and return your leg to the start position. After performing the desired number of reps, repeat the exercise with your left leg. To perform the move at home, attach weights to your ankles and perform the move as described.

At Home

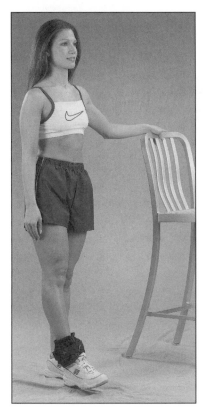 

SISSY SQUAT

Don't let the name fool you—this exercise definitely isn't for sissies! It's one of the best frontal thigh developers there is, especially for targeting the rectus femoris. Begin by taking a shoulder-width stance. Grasp a stationary object with one hand and rise up onto your toes. In one motion, slowly slant your torso back, bend your knees, and lower your body downward. Thrust your knees forward as you descend, and lean back until your torso is almost parallel with the floor. Then reverse direction and rise upward until you reach the start position.

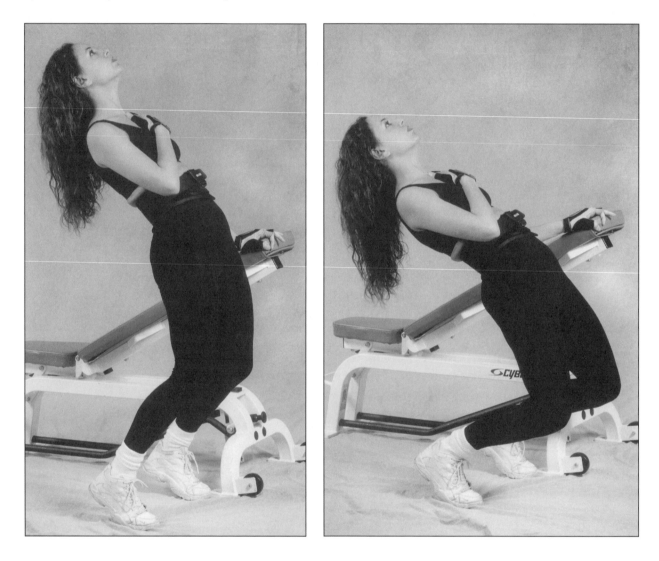

SIDE LUNGE

Begin by assuming a stance slightly wider than shoulder width. Grasp two dumbbells and hold one in front and one in back of your body. Keeping your left leg straight, slowly bend your left knee out to the side until your left thigh is parallel with the floor. Then slowly rise back up, and repeat immediately with your right knee bent out to the side.

QUADRICEPS EXERCISES

MACHINE ADDUCTION

Begin by sitting in an adductor machine with your legs spread apart, and place your inner thighs on the restraint pads. Slowly force your legs together, contracting your inner thighs as the pads touch one another. Then reverse direction and return to the start position.

LYING ADDUCTION

Although this is often regarded as a frivolous move by serious exercise enthusiasts, it can be very effective when performed with adequate intensity and properly integrated into a routine. Begin by lying down on your left side. Bring your right leg to the side of your body, bend it at a comfortable angle, and keep it elevated several inches off the ground. Keeping your left leg straight, slowly raise it as high as possible. Contract your inner thigh and return to the start position. After finishing the desired number of repetitions, turn over and repeat the exercise on your right side. For added intensity, attach ankle weights.

ADDUCTOR CABLE PULL

Begin by attaching a cuff to a low cable pulley and then securing the cuff to your right ankle. Position yourself so that your left side faces the weight stack, and grasp a sturdy portion of the machine for support. Slowly pull your left leg toward and across the midline of your body, as far to the right as possible. Contract your inner thigh muscles, and then reverse direction, returning your leg to the start position. After performing the desired number of reps, repeat the exercise with your right leg. To perform this move at home, attach a strength band to a stationary object and perform the move as described.

At Home

Victoria Johnson

My story: I began weight training in my teens during track season. I was a runner and I needed stronger legs. I quit during my college years and I started back in my mid-twenties to help me reshape my body. I was a cardio queen but I didn't have the physique I wanted. I found that you can't change your body shape without weight training. If you are a pear [shape] and you go on a diet and lose weight, you will just be a smaller pear. If you want a beautiful, symmetrically-shaped body, you must lift weights correctly.

Achievements: Northwest Aerobic Champion, National African American Dance Fitness Champion, Sculpting Video of the Year

©Dynamix Music

What do you consider your best fitness accomplishment?

Losing 60+ pounds and 20% body fat! I was 175+ lbs. and had 33% body fat. I was clinically obese and was afraid to step in front of a camera. Now I maintain a body fat of 12%.

How do you feel about using nutritional supplements?

With my busy video and TV schedule, I wouldn't dream of leaving home without my compact of supplements. I change my combinations depending on my goals. I take a series based on my filming schedule, another when I'm cutting fat, a third when I'm training for workshop series where I need a high cardio reserve, and another I use when I'm traveling for energy, healthy skin, recovery, and water retention.

What is your nutritional philosophy? Do you have a "power" food?

I am hypoglycemic, therefore I use the 50/30/20 plan—50% complex carbohydrates, 30% protein, and 20% fat. It has kept me lean, balanced, and healthy. My power food is protein smoothies with fresh fruit. They are quick, nutritious, and satisfy my sweet tooth!

What other types of physical activity do you do to diversify your fitness regimen?

I love to hip-hop dance and I volunteer at youth group outings where I use music and dance to introduce fitness to young kids. When I teach them about which muscles they are using to move in time with the music, they get really excited about their potential to take up other sports and eventually get into weight training.

How do you reward yourself after a great workout?

I relax with a great book! Knowing that I did something powerful for my body gives me the desire to do something powerful for my mind and soul as well.

Do you have any weight-training tips you'd like to pass on?

Keep your eye on the mirror. Work toward your perfect shape. Don't let anyone tell you anything that is contrary to how you want your body to look.

www.victoriajohnson.com

12

Lean Hamstrings and Glutes

Without question, women have more trouble firming up the backside than any other area of the body. This is the first place women tend to store fat, making it especially difficult to tone. Worse yet, this region is prone to cellulite, bringing about the dreaded "cottage cheese" appearance.

Training won't, by itself, reduce excess fat in your hamstrings and butt. As I noted earlier you cannot spot-reduce body fat. But by combining training with a proper nutritional regimen, you can sculpt these muscles to create an enviable posterior. If your butt is flat, you can shape it to give a rounded appearance. If your hamstrings are loose, you can tone them to achieve a rock-hard look. Regardless of your present condition, with a little hard work, a firm, shapely backside can be yours.

Bodysculpting Routine

You can activate the hamstrings at both the hip and knee joints but the glutes only at the hip. Thus, the hamstrings and glutes are classified into movements that train both muscle complexes together and exercises that target each complex individually.

• **Group 1**—stiff-legged dead lifts, back kicks, good mornings, hyperextensions, and similar variations. Although they use only one joint (the hip) in performance, these exercises are compound movements (movements using several different parts) in disguise. The lower back (spinal erectors), glutes, and hamstrings are all involved in their execution. To maximize the stress to the hamstrings and glutes, you must focus on contracting them on each repetition (although the lumbar muscles are still involved as stabilizers).

• **Group 2**—leg curls and similar variations. These movements focus on the hamstrings, with minimal stress on the glutes and lower back (the calves also play a small, secondary role in exercise performance). Leg curls provide several alternatives (standing, seated, kneeling, lying), and you can perform them using both legs together or one at a time.

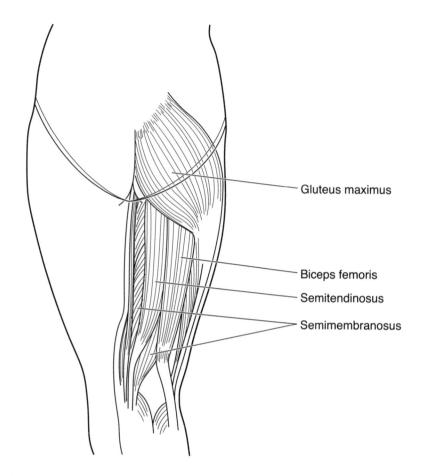

■ The gluteal and hamstring muscles.

• **Group 3**—abductor exercises and similar variations. These exercises focus on the glutes, with only minimal activation of the hamstrings. Abduction movements (that is, bringing your leg away from the midline of your body) target the gluteus medius and gluteus minimus, which are often overpowered by the much larger gluteus maximus. These exercises produce superior gluteal shape, giving your butt a tight, toned appearance.

Bodysculpting Tips

1. You should be careful doing any of the exercises in group 1 if you have previously injured your lower back. The muscles of the lower back (spinal erectors) are highly involved in the performance of these movements and can receive excessive stress, especially when you use weights. If this is a concern, you should employ unweighted versions of these movements (such as hyperextensions) that safely stimulate the hamstrings and glutes while simultaneously strengthening the muscles of the lower back.

2. To apply proper stress to your glutes, you must concentrate on contracting these muscles on every repetition. Women generally have difficulty understanding how to contract their glutes properly during exercise performance. If this is your concern, practice the movement without weights until it becomes second nature.

3. An excellent way to increase the muscle tone of the glutes is to supplement your training with butt squeezes (a method called isotension). This technique is both effective and extremely convenient. You can perform them almost anywhere, including when you are on the couch watching television, in line at the supermarket, or in bed before sleep. Simply contract your glute muscles, hold the squeeze for as long as possible (aim for 30 seconds or more), then release. After you are comfortable with the technique, try to do them in sets, counting each squeeze as one repetition. Perform three sets of 15 repetitions several times a week and you'll soon have buns of steel!

4. During open-chain hamstring exercises (leg curls and their variations), you can shift emphasis to various muscles of the hamstrings by varying your leg position. Turning your legs slightly outward (external hip rotation) targets the biceps femoris, while turning your legs slightly inward (internal hip rotation) works the semitendinosus and semimembranosus to a greater degree. Be careful, though, to stay within a comfortable range; excessive hip rotation when combined with intense knee flexion can lead to a joint-related injury.

TABLE 12.1 EXERCISES FOR THE HAMSTRINGS AND GLUTES

GROUP	EXERCISES
Group 1	Butt blaster
	Hyperextension
	Reverse hyperextension
	Cable back kick
	Good morning
	Stiff-legged dead lift
Group 2	Lying leg curl
	Seated leg curl
	Kneeling leg curl
	Standing cable leg curl
Group 3	Machine abduction
	Cable abductor pull
	Standing abduction
	Lying abduction

TABLE 12.2 SAMPLE TARGETED WORKOUTS FOR THE HAMSTRINGS AND GLUTES

WORKOUT	IN THE GYM		AT HOME	
	Exercise	**Sets**	**Exercise**	**Sets**
1	Hyperextension (p. 157) supersetted with lying leg curl (p. 162)	3	Stiff-legged dead lift (p. 161)	3
	Lying abduction (p. 169)	3	Standing cable leg curl (p. 165)	2
			Lying abduction (p. 169)	3
2	Stiff-legged dead lift (p. 161)	2	Reverse hyperextension (p. 158) supersetted with lying leg curl with ankle weights (p. 162)	3
	Standing cable leg curl (p. 165)	2	Cable abductor pull (p. 167)	2
	Machine abduction (p. 166)	3		
3	Good morning (p. 160)	3		
	Seated leg curl (p. 163) supersetted with standing abduction (p. 168)	2		
4	Reverse hyperextension (p. 158)	3		
	Kneeling leg curl (p. 164)	3		
	Cable abductor pull (p. 167)	2		

BUTT BLASTER

Begin by kneeling in a Butt Blaster™ machine. Place your forearms on the arm pads and your left foot on the footplate. Slowly push back your left leg; stop just short of locking your knee. Contract your glutes, and then reverse direction, slowly returning to the start position. Repeat with your right leg after finishing the desired number of reps with your left leg.

HYPEREXTENSION

Begin by lying prone in a Roman chair with your thighs resting on the restraint pad and your heels hooked under the rollers. Keep your hands across your chest and arch your lower back. Slowly raise your torso upward until it is just short of parallel with the floor. Contract your glutes, and then reverse direction, returning to the start position.

HAMSTRING AND GLUTE EXERCISES

REVERSE HYPEREXTENSION

Begin by lying face down on a flat bench with your lower body hanging off the end of the bench and your feet just short of touching the floor. Grasp the sides of the bench with both hands to support your body. Slowly raise your feet upward until they are just short of parallel with the ground, contracting your glutes at the top of the move. Then reverse direction and return your legs to the start position.

CABLE BACK KICK

Begin by attaching a cuff to a low cable pulley and to your right ankle. Face the weight stack and grasp a sturdy part of the machine for support. Slowly bring your right leg back as far as comfortably possible without moving your upper torso. Contract your glutes. Slowly return to the start position. Repeat with your left leg after finishing the desired number of reps with your right leg.

GOOD MORNING

Begin by resting a barbell across your shoulders, grasping the bar on both sides to keep it balanced. Assume a shoulder-width stance and keep your lower back taut throughout the movement. Slowly bend forward at the waist until your body is roughly parallel with the floor. In a controlled fashion, slowly reverse direction, contracting your glutes as you raise your body back to the start position.

STIFF-LEGGED DEAD LIFT

Begin by standing with your feet shoulder-width apart. Grasp a straight bar and let it hang in front of your body. Keeping your knees straight, slowly bend forward at the hips and lower the barbell until you feel an intense stretch in your hamstrings. Then reverse direction, contracting your glutes as you rise upward to the start position.

LYING LEG CURL

Begin by lying face down on a lying leg curl machine, with your heels hooked underneath the roller pads. Keeping your thighs pressed to the machine's surface, slowly lift your feet upward, stopping just short of touching your butt or as far as comfortably possible. Contract your hamstrings, and then reverse direction, returning to the start position. To increase stress to the hamstrings, choose a machine that permits a bend at the hips. To perform the move at home, attach ankle weights to both ankles. Lie down on a bench and perform the move as described.

At Home

SEATED LEG CURL

Begin by sitting in a seated leg curl machine and placing your heels over the roller pads. Lower the leg restraint over your thighs so that they are secure. Slowly press your feet downward as far as comfortably possible, contracting your hamstrings when your knees are fully bent. Then reverse direction and return to the start position.

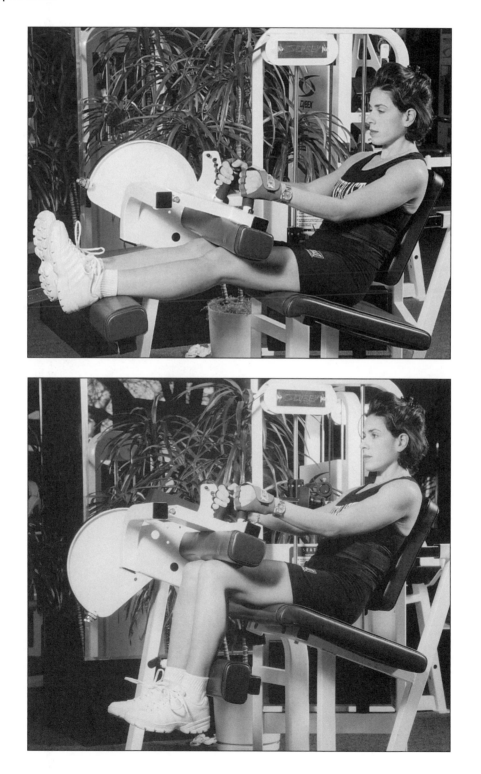

KNEELING LEG CURL

Begin by kneeling in a kneeling leg curl machine, placing your left heel underneath the roller pad. Place your forearms on the restraint pads for support. Slowly lift your left foot upward, stopping just short of touching your butt or as far as comfortably possible. Contract your left hamstring, and then reverse direction, returning to the start position. After performing the desired number of repetitions, repeat the exercise with your right leg.

STANDING CABLE LEG CURL

Begin by attaching a cuff to a low cable pulley and then securing the cuff to your right ankle. Position yourself so that you are facing the weight stack, and grasp a sturdy portion of the machine for support. Slowly flex your right knee, stopping just short of touching your butt with your foot or as far as comfortably possible. Contract your right hamstrings, and then reverse direction, returning to the start position. After performing the desired number of repetitions, repeat the exercise with your left leg. At home, attach a strength band to a stationary object and then fasten it to your ankle. Grab on to a stationary object and perform the move as described.

At Home

HAMSTRING AND GLUTE EXERCISES

MACHINE ABDUCTION

Begin by sitting in an abductor machine, and with your legs together, place your outer thighs on the restraint pads. Slowly force your legs apart as far as comfortably possible. Contract your glutes, and then reverse direction, returning to the start position.

CABLE ABDUCTOR PULL

Begin by attaching a cuff to a low cable pulley and then securing the cuff to your right ankle. Position yourself so that your left side faces the weight stack and grasp a sturdy portion of the machine for support. Pull your right leg across your left leg and directly out to the side. Contract your glutes, and then slowly return your leg along the same path back to the start position. After finishing the desired number of repetitions, invert the position and repeat with the left leg. To perform the move at home, attach a strength band to a stationary object and then fasten it to your ankle. Grab on to a stationary object and perform the move as described.

At Home

STANDING ABDUCTION

Begin by standing with your feet together and grasp a sturdy, stationary object for support. Bring your right leg directly out to the side as far as comfortably possible. Contract your glutes, and then slowly return your leg along the same path to the start position. After finishing the desired number of repetitions, repeat with the left leg. For added intensity, attach leg weights to your ankles.

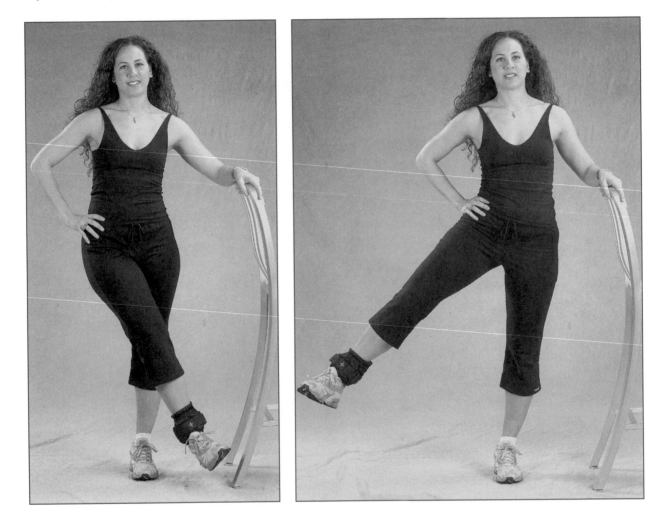

LYING ABDUCTION

Begin by lying down on your left side. Bend your left leg at a 90-degree angle and bring your left foot to rest underneath your right knee. Keeping your right leg straight, slowly raise it as high as possible. Contract your glutes, and return to the start position. After finishing the desired number of repetitions, turn over and repeat the process with your left leg. For added intensity, attach leg weights to your ankles.

13

Diamond Calves

In everyday life you use your calves more than any other muscle complex. You activate them every time you walk, run, climb stairs, or perform any other ambulatory movement. Whenever you are on your feet, your calves endure muscular stimulus.

Although the calves are frequently overlooked in the scheme of a training routine, diamond-shaped calves significantly augment your body lines. They contour your lower legs and complement the overall shape of your physique. In addition, they help create the illusion of leaner-looking thighs—a welcome side benefit for most women. Once you have developed these muscles, you'll see why diamonds really are a girl's best friend!

Bodysculpting Routine

Although the complete area of the lower leg contains ten small muscles, just two—the soleus and gastrocnemius—are the show muscles that most readily create optimal calf shape. Two basic positions are applicable for bodysculpting purposes: knees straight and knees bent. Exercises for the calves are classified by the amount of stress applied to each muscle.

• **Group 1**—standing calf raises, donkey calf raises, toe presses, and similar variations. These exercises use a straight-legged stance and thus place more stress on the gastrocnemius muscle. This is the largest of the calf muscles and the most important for aesthetic purposes.

• **Group 2**—seated calf raises and similar variations. These exercises require that you bend the knees, thereby emphasizing the soleus muscle. The soleus, for the most part, is hidden behind the gastrocnemius. When optimally developed, however, it adds fullness and shape to the calves. Most of the muscle fibers of the soleus (roughly 80 to 90 percent) are endurance oriented, making the soleus difficult to enhance through exercise.

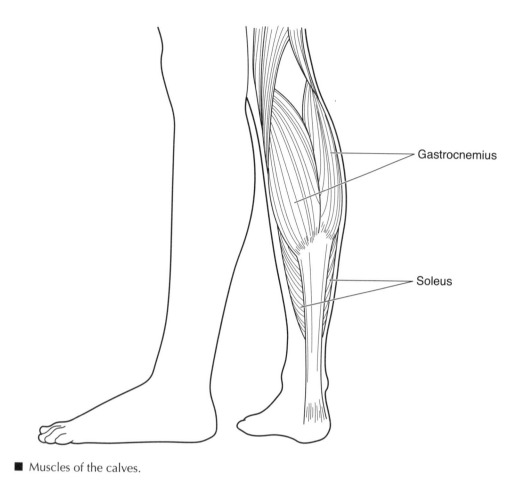

■ Muscles of the calves.

Bodysculpting Tips

1.   Contrary to popular belief, there is little benefit to turning your calves in or out during exercise performance. But by rolling onto the sides of your feet, you can shift the emphasis to different parts of the calf. Rolling your feet toward the big toes tends to stress the inner portion of the calf (medial head of the gastrocnemius). Alternatively, rolling toward your little toes emphasizes the outer aspect (lateral head of the gastrocnemius). Assess your calf development, and use this technique accordingly.

2.   Be careful to remain under control on the negative portion of any calf exercise. As your heel lowers to the floor, you stretch your Achilles tendon, applying a great deal of force to this area. You can severely injure your Achilles tendon if you are not careful, a potentially devastating event. Always lower slowly on the negative movement without bouncing, and stretch only to the point that the muscle allows.

3.   Because you use them in everyday activities, the calves are endurance-oriented muscles that respond stubbornly to training. Depending on genetics, the calves are often the most difficult muscles to shape. Accordingly, they can sometimes benefit from more repetitions than normal (as many as 30 per set). Because of the high percentage of endurance fibers in the soleus, a high number of repetitions can stimulate the muscle more effectively than other muscle groups, thereby improving results.

4. Make sure to stretch the calves between each set. Only one major artery feeds each of the calf muscles. (The sural artery feeds the gastrocnemius, and the posterior tibial artery feeds the soleus.) Thus, blood flow tends to be reduced to these muscles during training. This causes metabolic by-products such as lactic acid to accrue rapidly and increases the potential for muscular cramping. Stretching helps to flush the calves and decrease cramping, allowing better recuperation for your next set.

5. As with other muscles, you cannot alter the length of your calves through training. If your calf muscle is short and sits high on your lower leg, there is little you can do to increase its length (sorry, but that's the way it is). But by developing the soleus muscle (which extends into the lower region of the calf), you can add depth to the area, creating the impression of a longer muscle.

TABLE 13.1   EXERCISES FOR THE CALVES

GROUP	EXERCISES
Group 1	Machine toe press
	Donkey calf raise
	Toe press
	Standing calf raise
	One-leg standing calf raise
Group 2	Seated calf raise
	One-leg seated calf raise
	Bent-leg toe press

TABLE 13.2   SAMPLE TARGETED WORKOUTS FOR THE CALVES

WORKOUT	IN THE GYM		AT HOME	
	Exercise	Sets	Exercise	Sets
1	Donkey calf raise (p. 174)	3	One-leg standing calf raise (p. 177)	3
	One-leg seated calf raise (p. 177)	3	Seated calf raise (p. 178)	3
2	Machine toe press (p. 173)	3	Standing calf raise (p. 176)	3
	Bent-leg toe press (p. 180)	3	One-leg seated calf raise (p. 179)	3
3	Standing calf raise (p. 176)	3		
	Seated calf raise (p. 178)	3		
4	Donkey calf raise (p. 174) supersetted with toe press (p. 175)	3		
	One-leg seated calf raise (p. 179)	2		

MACHINE TOE PRESS

Begin by sitting in a toe press machine, pressing your back firmly into the padded seat. Place your toes at the bottom of the footplate a comfortable distance apart. Straighten your legs and drop your heels as far behind your toes as possible. Keeping your knees stable, slowly press your toes up as far as you can. Contract your calves, and then slowly reverse direction, returning to the start position.

CALF EXERCISES

DONKEY CALF RAISE

Begin by placing your middle back on the restraint pad of a donkey calf machine, keeping your lower back slightly arched at all times. Place the balls of your feet on the footplate and drop your heels below your toes. Slowly rise as high as you can onto your toes until your calves are fully flexed. Contract your calves, and then slowly reverse direction, returning to the start position.

TOE PRESS

Begin by sitting in a leg press machine, pressing your back firmly into the padded seat. Place your feet a comfortable distance apart, toes on the bottom of the footplate. Straighten your legs, unlock the carriage release bars, and drop your heels below your toes. Keeping your knees stable, slowly press your toes as high as you can. Contract your calves, and then slowly reverse direction, returning to the start position.

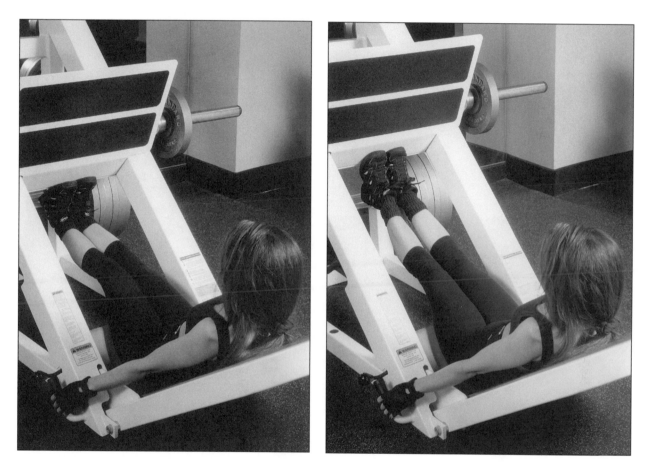

CALF EXERCISES

STANDING CALF RAISE

This is a standard move for targeting the gastrocnemius. Begin by placing your shoulders on the restraint pads of a standing calf machine. Place the balls of your feet on the footplate, and drop your heels below your toes. Slowly rise as high as you can onto your toes until your calves are fully flexed. Contract your calves, and then slowly reverse direction, returning to the start position. To do this move at home, begin by standing on a step (or staircase), heels past the edge, and allow your heels to drop below your toes. Hold onto a stationary object with one hand, and hold a dumbbell in the other hand. Perform the move as described.

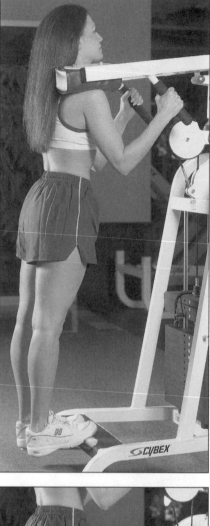

At Home

ONE-LEG STANDING CALF RAISE

Begin by placing your shoulders on the restraint pads of a standing calf machine. Place the ball of your right foot on the footplate, and drop your right heel below your toes. Slowly rise as high as you can onto your toes until your right calf is fully flexed. Contract your calf and then slowly reverse direction, returning to the starting position. Repeat with your left leg after finishing the desired number of reps with your right leg. To perform the move at home, grasp a stationary object in one hand and the dumbbells in another and perform as described.

At Home

CALF EXERCISES

SEATED CALF RAISE

This is the standard calf exercise for targeting the soleus. Begin by sitting in a seated calf machine, and place the restraint pads tightly across your thighs. Place the balls of your feet on the footplate, and drop your heels as far below your toes as possible. Slowly rise as high as you can onto your toes until your calves are fully flexed. Contract your calves, and then slowly reverse direction, returning to the start position. To perform this move at home, sit at the edge of a flat bench with your toes on a block of wood or step. Place a dumbbell on your thighs and hold it in place. Perform the move as described.

At Home

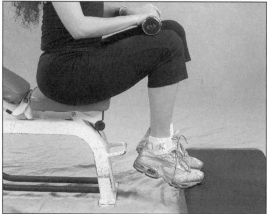

ONE-LEG SEATED CALF RAISE

Begin by sitting in a seated calf machine, and place the restraint pads tightly across your thighs. Place the balls of your right foot on the footplate, and drop your right heel as far below your toes as possible. Slowly rise as high as you can onto your toes until your right calf is fully flexed. Contract your calves, and then slowly reverse direction, returning to the start position. Repeat with your left leg.

At Home

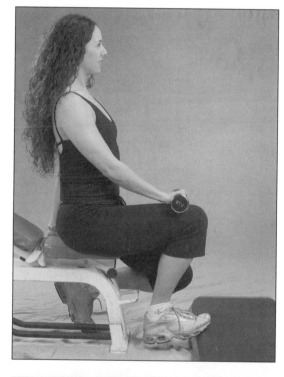

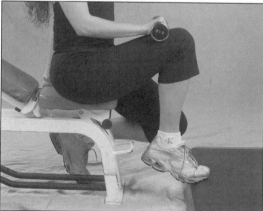

CALF EXERCISES

BENT-LEG TOE PRESS

This is a unique variation of the seated calf raise that can spice up your calf routine. Begin by sitting in a toe press machine, pressing your back firmly into the padded seat. Place your toes at the bottom of the footplate, feet a comfortable distance apart. Keep your knees bent at a 90-degree angle and drop your heels as far behind your toes as possible. Keeping your knees stable, slowly press your toes up as far as you can. Contract your calves, and then slowly reverse direction, returning to the starting position.

14

Six-Pack Abs

The abdominals are the showcase muscles of your physique. Because they reside in the center of your body, the abs are the first place that draws attention when you wear a bikini. Midriff shirts, crop tops, and similar garments are designed to flaunt this sensual area. For many women, however, a flat, toned stomach is elusive due to genetic factors.

Women tend to find the lower abdominal region extremely problematic. As I am sure you are aware, your menstrual cycle results in a significant amount of water retention each month. Your body adapts to this event by stretching the lower abs outward. Childbearing can further cause the area to spread. Because the lower portion of the rectus abdominis is much thinner than the upper portion, it can apply only limited resistance to nine months of distension. Therefore, the lower abs become soft and pliable, ultimately resulting in a slight pelvic bulge.

Despite these considerations, targeted bodysculpting can help you develop a great set of abs. Once you strip away abdominal body fat, it is rather easy to bring out detail in this region. With a dedicated routine, your midsection will readily take shape, achieving a toned, washboard appearance.

Bodysculpting Routine

The abdominals are one long sheath of muscle that runs from just below your breastbone (sternum) all the way down to your pelvis. Thus, you cannot separate the upper and lower abdominals or train one part without affecting the entire muscle. You can, however, apply more stress to the upper or lower abdominals by lifting from either the chest or the pelvis, respectively. Moreover, the sides of the midsection (obliques) are involved in various bending and twisting movements. Consequently, abdominal exercises are classified by whether they emphasize the upper or lower abdominal regions or the obliques.

• **Group 1**—crunches and similar variations. These movements put maximal stress on the upper portion of the abdominals. When executing crunches, you must concentrate on pulling your chest down toward your hips. Your lower back should never move; if it does, you activate your hip flexor muscles at the expense of your abdominals.

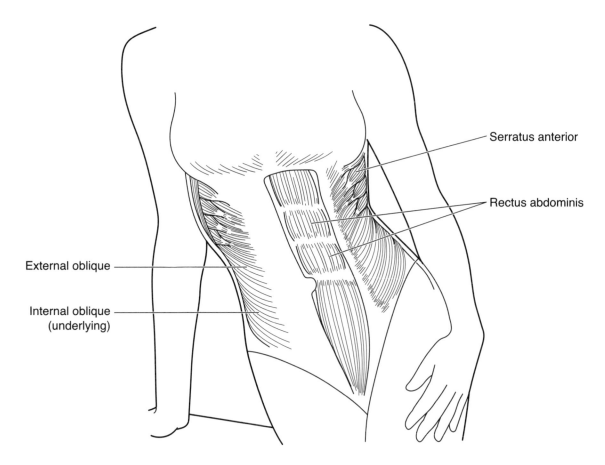

Serratus anterior

Rectus abdominis

External oblique

Internal oblique
(underlying)

■ Muscles of the abdomen.

• **Group 2**—leg raises, reverse crunches, and similar variations. These movements focus more on the lower portion of the abdominals. As noted, the lower abdominals are one of the most troublesome muscle groups for a woman to develop. Because of their anatomical position, they have limited range of motion, making it difficult to achieve a strong muscular contraction—a fact that seriously hampers your bodysculpting capabilities. To work the lower abs most effectively, it is imperative that you concentrate on raising your pelvis up toward your chest, not simply raising and lowering your legs. This minimizes hip flexor involvement and therefore maximizes stress to the lower abdominal region.

• **Group 3**—side bends, trunk twists, and similar variations. These movements target the internal and external obliques, the muscles that delineate your waist. When properly developed, the obliques provide the finishing touches to your midsection, giving your body a polished look.

Bodysculpting Tips

1. An effective way to train the abs is by performing your entire abdominal routine as a giant set. Because the abdominals are a flat sheath of muscle tissue, your ability to shape them is limited. Thus, your objective should be to achieve hardness in this area while shedding body fat to make the muscles visible. Decreased rest intervals increases the aerobic nature of the routine and therefore

helps to shed body fat. If possible, choose three exercises and move directly from one to the next, resting only long enough between sets to catch your breath.

2. When performing crunches, make sure to tuck your chin to your chest and put your hands across your body, not behind your head. You may tend to pull from the neck when your hands are behind your head, especially when you begin to approach failure. This not only reduces stress to your abdominals but also can strain the muscles in your neck.

3. If you have a naturally blocky waist, you should avoid training the obliques with all-out intensity. This is one area of the body where adding even a little bit of muscle can be detrimental to your overall proportions. Thus, evaluate your genetics and train these muscles accordingly.

4. Abdominal machines (such as the Gutbuster™) don't provide additional benefits over traditional exercises. They can, however, make the performance of these movements somewhat easier, which can be helpful if you have weak abdominal muscles. They are not a panacea, though, and won't make your stomach any flatter, as often advertised.

TABLE 14.1   EXERCISES FOR THE ABS

GROUP	EXERCISES
Group 1	Crunch
	Machine crunch
	Rope crunch
	Seated rope crunch
	Toe touch
Group 2	Reverse crunch
	Bench leg raise
	Hanging knee raise
	Leg lowering
Group 3	Side twist
	Twisting crunch
	Twisting, hanging leg raise
	Jackknife
	Reverse trunk twist

TABLE 14.2 SAMPLE TARGETED WORKOUTS FOR THE ABS

WORKOUT	IN THE GYM		AT HOME	
	Exercise	**Sets**	**Exercise**	**Sets**
1	Rope crunch (p. 187) supersettedwith bench leg raise (p. 191) and reverse trunk twist (p. 198)	3	Crunch (p. 185) supersetted with reverse crunch (p. 190) and jackknife (p. 197)	3
2	Crunch (p. 185) supersetted with hanging knee raise (p. 192) and jackknife (p. 197)	3	Toe touch (p. 189) supersetted with leg lowering (p. 193) and reverse crunch (p. 190)	3
3	Seated rope crunch (p. 188) supersetted with leg lowering (p. 193) and twisting, hanging leg raise (p. 196)	3		
4	Machine crunch (p. 186) supersetted with reverse crunch (p. 190) and twisting crunch (p. 195)	3		

CRUNCH

This is the standard move for targeting the upper abdominal region. Begin by lying face up on the floor with your feet planted firmly on the floor. Keep your knees bent to the ground or draped over a bench and your hands folded across your chest. Slowly raise your shoulders up and forward toward your chest, shortening the length of your trunk. Feel a contraction in the your abdominal muscles, and then slowly reverse direction, returning to the start position.

ABDOMINAL EXERCISES

MACHINE CRUNCH

Begin by lying face up in a crunch machine with your feet hooked underneath the restraint pads. Keep your thighs perpendicular to the ground and your hands folded across your chest. Slowly raise your shoulders up and forward toward your chest, shortening the length of your trunk. Feel a contraction in your abdominal muscles, and then slowly reverse direction, returning to the start position.

ROPE CRUNCH

This is my favorite abdominal movement. Begin by kneeling in front of a high pulley apparatus with your body facing the machine. Grasp a rope attached to the pulley and keep your elbows in toward your ears. Slowly curl your body downward, bringing your elbows to your knees. Contract your abs, and then slowly uncurl your body, returning to the start position.

SEATED ROPE CRUNCH

Follow the directions for rope crunches, except sit in a lat pull-down machine with your legs secured by the restraint pads. Grasp a rope attached to the pulley. Keeping your elbows close to your ears, slowly bring your elbows to your knees.

TOE TOUCH

Begin by lying flat on the floor with arms and legs straight up, perpendicular to your body. Slowly curl your torso up and forward, raising your hands as close to your toes as possible. Contract your abs, and then reverse direction, returning to the start position.

REVERSE CRUNCH

This is a terrific move for targeting the lower abs. Begin by lying back on a flat surface. Holding on to the sides of the bench, curl your knees in toward your stomach and raise your butt as high as possible while keeping your upper back pressed to the bench. Contract your abs, and then reverse direction, returning to the start position.

BENCH LEG RAISE

This is a decent preparatory move for more intense lower-abdominal movements. Due to extensive hip flexor involvement, however, you should move on to more focused abdominal exercises once you've developed sufficient strength in your abs. Sit at the edge of a flat bench. Lean back, keeping your upper torso at a 45-degree angle above the bench and your feet straight out and slightly below the bench. Maintaining a stable upper body, slowly raise your legs to a 45-degree angle with the floor. Contract your abs. Slowly lower your legs, returning to the start position.

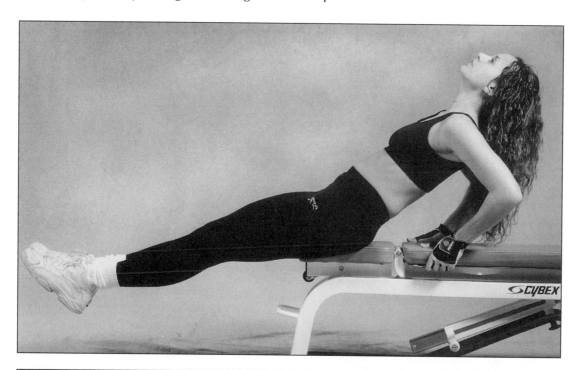

ABDOMINAL EXERCISES

HANGING KNEE RAISE

Begin by grasping a chinning bar with a shoulder-width grip and keep your upper torso motionless throughout the move. Keeping your knees bent, slowly raise your legs upward, lifting your butt so that your pelvis tilts toward your stomach. Contract your abs, and then reverse direction, returning your legs to the start position. For increased intensity, straighten your legs while performing the move. If you have trouble holding on to the bar, use arm straps for support.

LEG LOWERING

This is a difficult move to perform but if you can muster up the strength, the results are worth it. Begin by lying on the floor with your hands at your sides and feet together. Extend your legs toward the ceiling and bring your lower body off the floor, starting with your lower back and proceeding to your mid back. Breathe in at top of the move, and slowly roll back down in reverse sequence, exhaling as you descend.

SIDE TWIST

Begin by placing a bodybar, broomstick or similar implement behind your neck and allow it to rest across your shoulders. Wrap your arms around the bar and grasp each end to hold it in position. Slowly twist your upper body to the right as far as possible, contracting your oblique muscles as you turn. Then reverse direction and twist your body all the way to the left in the same fashion. Only your waist should move during this maneuver; keep your hips stationary at all times. To reduce torque to your neck, look straight ahead and do not allow your neck to turn during exercise performance.

TWISTING CRUNCH

This is an excellent overall ab move that focuses on the obliques. Begin by lying face up on the floor with your calves resting on top of a flat bench. Your thighs should be perpendicular to the ground and your hands should be folded across your chest. Slowly raise your shoulders up and forward toward your chest, twisting your body to the right. Feel a contraction in your abdominal muscles, and then slowly reverse direction, returning to the start position. After performing the desired number of repetitions on the right, repeat the process, twisting your body to the left.

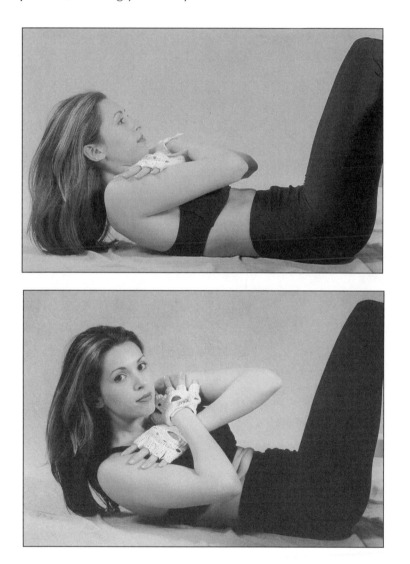

ABDOMINAL EXERCISES

TWISTING, HANGING LEG RAISE

Begin by grasping a chinning bar with a shoulder-width grip, and keep your upper torso motionless throughout the move. Keeping your knees bent, slowly raise your legs upward and to the right, lifting your butt so that your pelvis tilts toward your stomach. Contract your abs and obliques, and then reverse direction, returning your legs to the start position. After performing the desired number of repetitions to the right, repeat the process, raising your legs to the left. If you have trouble holding on to the bar, use arm straps for support.

JACKKNIFE

Begin by lying on your left side with your feet together. Make a fist with your right hand and keep it pressed to your right ear. Raise your torso toward your right leg as far as possible. Contract your oblique muscles, and then slowly reverse direction and return to the start position. After performing the desired number of repetitions on the right, repeat the exercise on the left.

REVERSE TRUNK TWIST

Begin by lying on your back with your arms out to the sides and palms on the floor. Keeping your legs straight and feet together, raise your legs so that they are perpendicular with the ground. Slowly lower your legs directly to the right, keeping your torso pressed to the floor throughout the move. Raise your legs back to the start position, and repeat on your left. Alternate from side to side for the desired number of repetitions.

Nicole Rollolazo

My story: I am a petite woman (only 4'11"), so being physically fit and strong is definitely a confidence booster—knowing that I have a better chance of protecting myself. It also makes me feel better about myself and my health. Before I started getting serious about weight training, I had a "little girl's body." Now I have more shape and it makes me feel better about the way I look.

Achievements: 2000 Fitness America Pageant Champion

© www.Alexardenti.com

What motivated you to begin a weight-training program? How old were you when you started?

Since age 4 I was involved in gymnastics and dance. I had to start weight training for gymnastics about 9. My high school held a bodybuilding competition and after winning that I was hooked!

How do you feel about using nutritional supplements?

I think supplements are a must. It is extremely hard to give your body what it needs to achieve the type of muscle fitness competitors build through food alone.

What is your nutritional philosophy? Do you have a "power" food?

I believe it is important to eat clean, but I also think you can't be obsessed with a healthy diet. Cheat meals are important to keep you sane! My power food is my oatmeal for breakfast.

What other types of physical activity do you do to diversify your fitness regimen?

Kickboxing, snowboarding, dancing, and rock climbing.

How do you reward yourself after a great workout?

I love a nice long bubble bath to soothe my muscles and relax.

Do you have any training tips you'd like to pass on?

A lot of women believe they will get bulky if they use weights, but the truth is that it takes years and years of hardcore weight training and diet to achieve the type of muscles that bodybuilders and fitness competitors have. By building some muscle it will help increase your metabolism.

www.nicolefitness.com

15

Fat Burning With Aerobics

For the majority of women, aerobics are synonymous with exercise. Many have never attempted any type of weight training, but most have taken part in some form of aerobic exercise.

Unfortunately, aerobics are often misunderstood. There is a prevailing misconception that aerobics are the key to physical perfection: just get on the treadmill or take a few classes and you'll turn your body into a work of art, right? Wrong! You won't achieve desired results simply by throwing together a cardio routine. To obtain proper benefits, you must assess your needs and appropriately integrate aerobics into your fitness program. Proper, scientifically determined implementation of cardiovascular activities can have a profound impact on your overall results.

Simply stated, an aerobic exercise is any activity that requires your body to use oxygen (as opposed to anaerobic exercise, which does not consume oxygen). Oxygen use is generally accompanied by a corresponding elevation in resting heart rate and an increase in vascular blood flow. From a bodysculpting perspective, aerobics serves a dual purpose: it improves muscular endurance and decreases fat stores. Aerobics complements your weight-training regimen, working synergistically to help you achieve total fitness.

Bodysculpting Benefits of Aerobics

Although the health benefits of cardiovascular exercise are well known, the way in which it interacts with the bodysculpting process is not as well understood. Besides realizing that it helps burn calories, most women have a poor comprehension of the effect that aerobics has on their physiques. To get a better handle on the way that cardio affects your bodysculpting endeavors, let's explore its benefits.

- **Fat burning.** Cardiovascular exercise expedites fat burning. A large percentage of the calories that are expended during aerobic training are derived from fat. Depending on your exercise intensity, a single session of cardio can burn more than 20 grams of fat—enough to offset the amount in a greasy burger and fries. But the fat-burning effects extend beyond the immediate ones. Your metabolism remains elevated even after you have finished training, prolonging fat burning for up to several hours after your session. Moreover, your mitochondria (cellular furnaces where fat burning takes place) expand in size and number, and your aerobic enzymes (proteins that accelerate the fat-burning process) increase in quantity. Over time, these factors allow your body to rely more on fat than glycogen (carbohydrates) for fuel, helping long-term weight management.

• **Muscular endurance.** Cardiovascular exercise promotes better muscular endurance for weight training. When you lift weights, your body converts glucose into the high-energy compound ATP (through a process called glycolysis) to fuel exercise performance. During this conversion process, lactic acid is produced and rapidly accumulates in your muscles as you train. When lactic acid builds up past a certain point, you experience an intense burning sensation in your muscles. Ultimately, the burn becomes so strong that it inhibits your ability to continue training. However, when you increase your aerobic capacity, your cardiovascular system becomes more efficient at delivering oxygen to your working muscles. This helps to increase your lactate threshold—the point at which there is more lactic acid in your body than can be metabolized—and thereby delays the onset of lactic acid buildup. The end result is a greater capacity to train at high-energy levels.

• **Muscular recuperation.** Cardiovascular exercise aids in muscular recuperation. Aerobics help to expand your network of capillaries, the tiny blood vessels that allow nutrients such as protein and carbohydrates to be absorbed into body tissues. The more capillaries that you have, the more efficient your body becomes in utilizing these nutrients for muscular repair. Capillaries also help to clear waste products, particularly carbon dioxide, from the food-burning process, further enhancing the efficiency of your nutrient delivery system. This accelerates the rate at which your muscles are able to get the resources needed for recuperation, helping to improve workouts and speed recovery.

Sex Differences in Aerobics

Although the benefits of cardio exercise are numerous, achieving them is decidedly more complicated. Women in general are at a particular disadvantage regarding aerobic training. Several distinct sex differences influence overall aerobic ability, and women regrettably get the short end of the stick. Unlike many differences between the sexes, these discrepancies are rather subtle. But to enjoy a safe and effective workout, you must consider these differences when constructing your aerobic routine. Following are some inherent sex differences in aerobic performance.

• A woman's aerobic capacity is roughly 10 to 20 percent lower than a man's. Women generally have smaller internal organs (including the heart and lungs) as well as lower hemoglobin levels than men. This results in lower cardiac output (the amount of blood pumped out of the heart in one minute), which curtails a woman's ability to deliver blood and oxygen to exercising muscles. Because oxygen is required to sustain aerobic exercise, women's endurance is less than men's. Moreover, the heart and lungs help expel metabolic waste from the body, aiding in the recovery process. Because these organs are smaller in women, they do not remove waste as efficiently, thereby reducing their recuperative ability. The net effect is that women have to work harder than men to achieve the same level of aerobic fitness.

■ Be careful when performing high impact aerobics.

©bachmann

• Women have a greater potential for joint and connective tissue injury than men. Women tend to have small bone structures that are highly susceptible to the rigors of training. Aerobic exercise can heighten the demands placed on the joints and connective tissue, making them more prone to injury. The knees are especially vulnerable because of a woman's large Q-angle (the angle formed between the knee and the outer thigh). As a rule, the wider the hips, the greater the Q-angle. Because women have wider hips (to accommodate the demands of childbirth), they ordinarily have larger Q-angles. Larger Q-angles cause greater force to be placed on the knees during strenuous activities, substantially increasing the potential for injury to this area. Thus, women must be particularly careful when performing endurance activities that are ballistic in nature (for example, step classes and high-impact aerobics).

• Hormonal fluctuations can compromise women's aerobic ability. Prolonged exercise can cause dizziness, nausea, and other side effects during menstruation and menopause. Hormonal imbalances during these periods throw off the body's normal rhythms, resulting in a variety of symptoms. This impedes cardiovascular capacity and makes training more difficult. Moreover, the general discomfort that some women experience can further reduce their training motivation. Some women must cope with difficult symptoms such as cramps and headaches, magnifying the importance of discipline.

Aerobic Myths

Further complicating the quest for aerobic fitness is the rampant misinformation that abounds in fitness circles. Somehow, numerous myths relating to cardiovascular exercise have been taken as gospel. By sifting through this misinformation, you'll develop a better understanding of how to integrate cardio into your routine. To get the most out of your efforts, let's dispel some of the more common myths and explore the realities of aerobics.

MYTH   Using the stair climber gives you a big butt.

This myth gained credence when a popular magazine suggested that the stair climber was responsible for increasing the derrieres of exercising women across the country. Afraid that they would soon possess a rear end the size of a movie screen, women began to avoid the stair climber like the plague. The fact is, though, there isn't a shred of truth to this myth. It's virtually impossible to increase muscle mass substantially through the performance of any cardiovascular activity. The reason for this is simple: there are two basic types of muscle fibers, slow-twitch (type I) and fast-twitch (type II), and each responds to different stimuli.

Fast-twitch fibers are strength-related fibers that contract rapidly but are quick to fatigue. They derive most of their energy from burning glycogen, rather than fat, as a fuel source. These factors make them more sensitive to intense weight-bearing exercises (such as push-ups, squats, and so on) performed over short time periods. To accommodate the demands of anaerobic exercise, fast-twitch fibers respond by growing larger and stronger. They are the only types of fibers that can significantly increase in size and promote muscular bulk.

Slow-twitch fibers, on the other hand, are endurance-oriented fibers that have limited ability to grow larger. These fibers get much of their energy by burning fat for fuel; they contract slowly but are able to endure extended periods of activity. Slow-twitch fibers are predominantly used during the performance of aerobic exercise, with almost no activation of fast-twitch fibers particularly without an overload. Little, if any, muscular growth can take place in the slow-twitch fibers. Because exercising on the stair climber is aerobic, it stands to reason that it cannot contribute to building substantial muscle tissue in any part of the body, including your butt!

MYTH   You can't overtrain by performing cardiovascular exercise.

Because aerobics are an endurance activity executed at decreased intensity, many women feel that there is no limit to how much they can perform. However, although your body can tolerate a greater volume of cardiovascular exercise than anaerobic activity, too much of it will eventually set back your fitness endeavors and have a negative impact on your physique.

Although recovery ability varies among individuals, your body needs rest and recuperation to regenerate its glycogen stores. Glycogen reserves are your body's primary short-term energy source, giving you the strength and endurance to perform everyday chores. Because cardio exercise burns glycogen (as well as fat), too much cardio exercise depletes these reserves, ultimately causing you to become overtrained.

Overtraining makes your body less efficient in using fat for fuel and is apt to feed on your muscle tissue for energy (due to secretion of stress hormones). Moreover, it can throw off your biochemical balance, resulting in a variety of complications, including cessation of your period (amenorrhea), constant fatigue, and other anomalies. Therefore, you must pay keen attention to symptoms of overtraining and modify your aerobic activity according to your physical state.

MYTH   Low-intensity aerobic activities are better for fat burning than high-intensity exercise.

This myth was given credence when several research studies indicated that low-intensity activities burned a greater percentage of fat calories than high-intensity activities. These studies confirmed that the body prefers to use fat as its fuel source during low-intensity exercise (using fat for roughly 60 percent of the calories burned, as opposed to about 40 percent during high-intensity exercise).

It is misguided, however, to believe that the selective use of fat for fuel translates into burning more total fat calories. High-intensity exercise burns more absolute fat calories than lower-intensity activities. And because the most important aspect of fat burning is the total number of fat calories burned—not the percentage from fat—higher-intensity exercise has the decided edge.

Furthermore, when you consider time spent training, low-intensity exercise provides a poor cost–benefit dividend. After all, why would you want to spend an hour running on the treadmill when you can get better results by exercisingfor half that time? In final analysis, if fat burning is your aim, performing cardiovascular exercise at a higher intensity is the more efficient choice.

MYTH   Sweat is a good indicator of exercise intensity.

Most women mistakenly believe that you "gotta sweat" to have a successful workout. But while sweat is usually associated with rigorous exercise, it is by no means essential to achieving results.

When you exercise, sweat is brought on by an elevation of body temperature from metabolic heat. Your body regulates its temperature by activating your sweat glands, which then release water through your pores as a cooling mechanism. Thus, sweat is an indicator that your body temperature is rising, not necessarily that you are exercising at an intense level. Rather than judging your workout by how much you sweat, use maximal heart rate or maximal oxygen consumption as a yardstick of how hard you are working.

Moreover, contrary to popular belief, being out of shape does not increase your propensity to sweat. In fact, the more physically fit you are, the more you tend to perspire. Frequent exercise makes your sweat glands increasingly sensitive to rises in body temperature. Over time, your body begins to perceive the start of exercise and, not wanting to store extra heat, signals the sweat glands sooner than it did before you began your training program.

MYTH   Aerobics classes are the best form of cardiovascular exercise.

Mention aerobics and most people envision an instructor leading a class through various jumps, twists, and other athletic movements. Every week there seems to be a new gimmick with a catchy name and a clever marketing angle: high impact, step, slide, spin . . . the list is seemingly endless. Without question, aerobics classes can be fun. They provide a festive atmosphere with lively music and dance-oriented maneuvers. They also can be a great place to socialize and meet new people, adding to the experience. For those who are not internally motivated to exercise, these factors can provide an impetus to become more active.

Generally speaking, however, you are better off performing individual aerobic modalities rather than participating in group classes. Group-oriented activities have several drawbacks. First, by catering to the masses, it is unlikely that a class will specifically target your specific abilities. Second, because of the extreme, unorthodox nature of the movements involved in many classes, the risk of sustaining an injury is much greater in this setting. So if you're looking for optimal results, this really isn't the best way to go.

In contrast, individual aerobic modalities let you train within your own abilities. You can customize a routine to meet your specific needs, thereby maximizing your fat-burning potential. And because individual modalities are executed in a controlled fashion, they tend to be much safer to perform.

In final analysis, if you simply cannot motivate yourself to exercise or just want to have some fun, an aerobics class might be right for you. But if you're looking for maximal results in minimal time, an individualized cardio program is the better choice. And while anything that helps to increase your motivation to exercise is worthwhile, experience has shown that the best way to encourage lasting adherence is to achieve results in the safest, most expedient way possible. There is no greater motivating factor than seeing your body change before your eyes!

Philosophy of Aerobic Training

To achieve optimal results, it's also important to appreciate the philosophical differences between the aerobic and weight-training components of the High-Energy Fitness system. Although weight training in a high-energy format provides aerobic benefits, it is still largely an anaerobic endeavor. Weight training requires short bouts of intense training with all-out effort, culminating in muscular failure. This breaks down muscle and connective tissue and overloads your central nervous system. Because of the tremendous stress to your body, you must maintain a set schedule that provides adequate rest to regenerate bodily function.

Cardiovascular exercise, on the other hand, is an endurance activity (that is, an activity performed continuously for relatively long periods of time). Compared with weight training, the intensity of these activities is moderate. The goal in aerobics isn't to overload your muscles, but rather to sustain an elevated heart rate for the duration of training. Only minimal breakdown of muscle tissue is associated with aerobics, permitting rapid recuperation from an exercise session. Therefore, you can perform cardio exercise more frequently than weight training, with less recovery time between sessions.

Aerobic Training Protocol

In order to get the most out of the cardiovascular component of this system, adhere to the following protocol:

- **Frequency.** How often you engage in aerobic exercise depends on your genetics and overall activity level. Most women should perform cardio exercise three to five days a week, but personal circumstances may require varying these guidelines. Assess factors such as your general muscular conditioning and your need to lose additional body fat, and adjust the frequency of your aerobic training accordingly. As stated earlier, high-energy weight training seriously taxes your body's resources, including your muscles, connective tissue, and central nervous system. Aerobic exercise can compound this predicament. To avoid overtraining, I recommend that you give your body at least two days a week of complete rest from exercise. Limiting cardio exercise to no more than five sessions per week helps to regenerate your energy supplies and to enhance recuperation. Remember, more is not necessarily better. Too much aerobic activity can cause your body to break down muscle tissue for fuel. Ultimately, this leads to a decrease in muscle tone and a slowdown of your metabolic system—the opposite of the effect you seek.

WEIGHT TRAINING FOR WEIGHT LOSS

Weight training helps to promote fat loss and is arguably even more important than aerobics in long-term weight management. You see, muscle is metabolically active tissue. For each pound of muscle that you gain, your body burns an additional 50 calories a day at rest. Thus, by putting on a mere five pounds of muscle (something that a novice trainee can accomplish in a few months), you'll burn an additional 250 calories a day, even while lying on your couch reading a book! Better yet, most of the resting energy is derived from fat, so you ultimately will tap into those hard-to-reduce areas.

People tend to restrict their caloric intake while trying to lose weight. But this causes the body to enter a starvation mode and begin to catabolize (break down) muscle tissue for fuel. If you neglect weight training, your metabolism will begin to slow down from the loss of muscle. This produces a rebound effect after you no longer restrict your calorie intake, and you ultimately can gain back even more weight than you lost by dieting.

- **Duration.** You don't need to perform lengthy aerobic sessions to reduce body fat. I've seen women stay on the treadmill for hours on end. They are so consumed with losing weight that cardiovascular exercise takes up a significant portion of their day. However, not only is this unnecessary, it actually can be counterproductive. As long as you train properly, optimal results are achieved in a modicum of time. During the initial stages of training, you may be able to endure only a few minutes of cardio. If you aren't aerobically conditioned, oxygen will be in short supply, and you'll get winded rather easily. Don't let this get you down. Endurance tends to build up rapidly. Within a few weeks, you'll see major improvements in your stamina, and before long, cardio will be a breeze. Once you have built up sufficient endurance, your total aerobic activity should last a minimum of about 20 minutes. Recent evidence suggests that you can break this amount into several smaller bouts of exercise and still achieve the same benefit as performing one longer aerobic session. On the other hand, there are diminishing returns to performing cardio for extended periods of time. Lengthy, drawn-out aerobic sessions take a toll on your body and can easily lead to overtraining. Thus, to avoid any negative consequences, limit your sessions to no more than about 45 minutes. By keeping the duration of your sessions between these prescribed boundaries, you'll maximize fat burning while mitigating any potential risk.

- **Intensity.** Although there are many ways to measure aerobic intensity, one of the easiest and most effective methods is percentage of maximal heart rate (220 minus your age). Using this method, you should perform cardiovascular exercise at a stable pulse of 50 to 80 percent of your maximal heart rate. Be sure to begin with a brief warm-up at low intensity, and finish with a cool-down at a similar level. As you progress in your training endeavors, you should attempt to elevate the intensity of your aerobic sessions until you are training at close to 80 percent of your maximal heart rate. Not only does this allow you to accomplish more in less time, but it also helps condition your cardiovascular system to raise your lactate threshold.

- **Variation.** As with the weight-training component of this system, you should vary your aerobic routine, cross-training among several different aerobic modalities (bike, treadmill, stair climber, and so forth). Cross-training, an essential concept in cardiovascular exercise, helps reduce boredom and promotes adherence to your routine. You can best accomplish cross-training by alternating modalities from one workout to the next, never allowing your body to become accustomed to a particular exercise. In this way, you keep your body off guard, preventing specific adaptation. Moreover, because you use different muscles in exercise performance, your joints aren't subjected to continual impact, significantly reducing the likelihood of injury. All told, cross-training should be an integral part of your cardiovascular regimen.

Cardiovascular Protocol

Frequency:	3 to 5 days a week
Duration:	20 to 45 minutes per session
Intensity:	50% to 80% of maximal heart rate
Variation:	Alternate among several exercise modalities

The cardiovascular protocol summarizes the High-Energy Fitness protocol for cardiovascular training. As with weight training, proper application of this protocol determines your results. Because your aerobic routine will have an impact on your weight-training program, striking the right balance between the two is essential in optimizing your physique. I advise you to proceed cautiously, starting with the minimum recommended levels and advancing with care. Although your inclination may be to go all out, you can run the risk of pushing too far. There is a fine line between training and overtraining, and only prudence can prevent you from crossing over it.

Choosing Aerobic Modalities

Now that you know how to incorporate aerobics appropriately into your routine, you face another dilemma: which specific exercises should you perform for best results? Fitness experts have hotly debated this issue, and many have proposed this or that particular exercise as the "best." There is such a wide range of aerobic modalities available that the consumer is literally overwhelmed with options. Making matters worse, new types of cardiovascular machines are continually flooding the market. Marketers use fancy infomercials to promote these products, often hiring a celebrity to claim that theirs is the "ultimate fat-burning vehicle." With all the hype surrounding these machines, how do you separate fact from fiction?

In truth, when all factors are considered, there is not much difference in total calories burned among aerobic modalities. Table 15.1 lists the approximate caloric expenditure for some of the more common aerobic activities. Note that the figures listed are for calories burned per hour. If you were to perform an activity for a half hour, a more reasonable duration, the difference between exercises is even less significant.

At first glance, it would seem that the treadmill is the aerobic exercise of choice. After all, it burns the most calories of all the modalities. These figures, however, don't take into account the body's propensity for adaptation, which greatly influences caloric expenditure. As previously noted, the human body readily adjusts to external stimuli by becoming more proficient in the activity, constantly improving its efficiency. The only way to counteract this is by continually increasing the intensity of the activity—a course that has a limited ceiling. Hence, using the treadmill exclusively inevitably leads to diminished returns. As detailed in the protocol, cross-training among exercises is the only way to avoid this phenomenon, and cross-training therefore yields the best results. Despite the

TABLE 15.1   CALORIC EXPENDITURE FOR SELECTED AEROBIC ACTIVITIES

ACTIVITY	CALORIES PER HOUR	
	MODERATE	VIGOROUS
Bike with arms	255	355
Cross-country ski machine	298	339
Rowing machine	303	370
Stair climber	314	373
Stationary bike	249	302
Treadmill	353	433

hype, there simply is no single best exercise; using the treadmill, or any other modality, to the exclusion of other activities is counterproductive.

A good way to boost aerobic intensity is to incorporate rhythmic arm movements into the activity. When you swing your arms back and forth at shoulder level, your heart pumps blood against the force of gravity, increasing oxygen consumption and burning additional calories. To further accelerate calorie burning, you can hold hand weights while you train. It has been shown that walking at four miles per hour with hand weights burns the same number of calories as running at five miles per hour, with a 50 percent decrease in joint compression forces!

As for all exercises, the safety of an aerobic modality is of paramount importance. Many potential pitfalls are associated with specific activities, and avoiding them is critical for you to remain injury free. Because women are especially prone to joint-related ailments, this consideration is of particular consequence.

One area of concern involves aerobics classes. As recommended earlier, you should, for the most part, avoid them. These classes are not only inferior in their ability to burn calories, but also dramatically heighten the potential for injury. Instead, use cardiovascular machines such as the treadmill, stationary bike, stair climber, and so on whenever possible. Taking all factors into account, these machines provide an excellent risk–reward balance and are the modalities of choice for aerobic training.

Running presents another potential hazard. More than any type of cardio exercise, running can have a debilitating effect on your shins and knees. Studies have shown that frequent runners have up to a 70 percent rate of injury to the lower extremities. These risks are magnified when you run on the street or on a paved surface, which exacerbates stress on your joints. Moreover, potholes, wet leaves, and snow present additional hazards, heightening the possibility of serious injury.

If you choose to run or jog, I recommend that you do so on a high-quality treadmill. A treadmill has a cushioned surface that absorbs some of the stress on your shins and knees. Although this doesn't completely eliminate ground reaction forces, the overall impact is alleviated. As a side benefit, the treadmill forces you to regulate your speed, keeping your heart rate constant. If you simply cannot resist running outdoors, do so on a track specifically designed for this purpose. In addition, consider wearing a knee brace for extra support and stabilization. Your legs will thank you!

Swimming is a poor choice as a fat burner because water temperature is well below your normal body temperature (unless you swim in a hot tub). Swimming causes your body to struggle to preserve its internal heat. Over time, your body responds by developing an insulating layer of fat. Therefore, from a bodysculpting perspective, swimming should be enjoyed only on an occasional basis.

Regardless of which modalities you choose, you must be careful to maintain your focus while training aerobically. As opposed to weight training, cardio exercise tends to promote injuries of indiscretion. Because you perform weight training for brief intervals at high intensity, you must focus on the activity at hand. A set lasts only a minute, and it is easy to maintain your concentration throughout the lift. On the other hand, aerobic sessions can go on for extended periods, and letting your mind wander can help pass the time, encouraging sloppiness in training and increasing the chance of injury. Be smart: pay attention to your form, and don't get careless!

When to Perform Aerobics

An often-asked question concerns the timing of cardiovascular exercise: should it be done at the beginning or at the end of your workout? Many women like to perform aerobics when they first get to the gym, while others prefer to wait until they have finished training with weights. Although both alternatives are acceptable, a good case can be made for performing your cardio workout after your weight-training session. Several benefits substantiate this line of reasoning.

First, aerobics serve as an active form of recovery, helping to flush lactate from your muscles. This metabolic by-product is what causes the "burn" in your muscles and impairs muscular contractions. By the time you finish a high-energy weight-training session, a great deal of lactate has accrued within your muscles. Performing submaximal cardio exercise after lifting can help remove these by-products, thereby enhancing muscular recuperation.

Second, because weight training requires much higher intensity than aerobics, you need more energy for exercise performance. By training with weights when your energy reserves are high, you can go all out in your lifting efforts. As energy levels dissipate, your weight-training ability wanes, and your capacity to train effectively is compromised. Alternatively, because cardio exercise requires less than all-out intensity, the timing of performance is of less consequence. Within reason, your aerobic ability should not be substantially affected by when you exercise.

Last, if you become fatigued or are pressed for time, you can postpone your cardio routine without repercussions. Your body can recuperate much more quickly from aerobics than from weight training, allowing you greater flexibility with the timing of your cardiovascular regimen. As long as you get in an appropriate number of workouts per week, the structure of the routine is of little consequence. Because cardio exercise can be performed several days in a row without ill effect, you can have the luxury of deviating from your regular schedule to accommodate your needs.

Although these factors suggest that it is more beneficial to save cardio exercise until the end of your workout, the overall impact of timing is modest. If you have good cardiovascular capacity, you can achieve good results either way. I recommend that you experiment with both methods and assess the effect on your workouts. Listen to your body, and then make your decision on this issue. If you are more comfortable performing your cardio workout first, then, of course, go for it!

Tanja Baumann

My story: True confidence is about you and not just your body. Whatever your reflection in the mirror, you are always the same person and our bodies are just our tools for a healthy life. Treat your body as home you want to live and feel comfortable in. Don't try to control your body too much. You're beautiful! Use fitness as a way of life.

Achievements: Miss Millennium 2002, 1998 Aerobics Fitness World Champion

©Tanja Baumann

What motivated you to begin a weight-training program? How old were you when you started?

After a few years in classical ballet when I was about 4 years old, I got into jazz, then aerobics (as an instructor) and began weight training due to my scoliosis and passion for higher personal physical fitness achievements.

How do you feel about using nutritional supplements?

Never have—don't now—and never want to.

Do you have a "power" food?

Chocolate! Especially Swiss chocolate. Lots of it!

What other types of physical activity do you do to diversify your fitness regimen?

I teach a wide variety of classes such as cardio kickboxing, salsa, hip-hop, body pump, step, kids dance, and I love to swim and go for long walks in nature.

How do you reward yourself after a great workout?

Being able to train hard and pain-free is reward enough. Of course, I always enjoy my food at the end of the day!

Do you have any training tips you'd like to pass on?

Train every part of your body, whatever your shape or size. Focus on each muscle group and concentrate. Keep your workouts short (max. 1 hour) but intense and enjoy feeling strong!

www.tanja-baumann.ch

16

Safe Workouts During Pregnancy

Pregnancy can be one of the most exhilarating experiences known to a woman, but its effects on the body can also make it one of the most demoralizing. As a personal trainer, I often hear from women who have had babies that they cannot lose their pregnancy weight after giving birth. And it's no wonder. During pregnancy, women undergo many physiological and hormonal changes that can drastically alter metabolism and physical conditioning.

Benefits of Exercise During Pregnancy

Unfortunately, many women still believe that pregnancy requires a sedentary lifestyle. Fearing that strenuous activity will threaten their well-being, they become couch potatoes. Even worse, some train haphazardly while pregnant, jeopardizing not only their health but that of their fetus as well. There are so many misconceptions about training during pregnancy that many obstetricians are not sure how to counsel their patients on this subject. Yet a properly implemented exercise regimen can provide many positive effects for pregnant women with virtually no risk. You can derive the following benefits from a well-executed training routine.

• **Less likelihood of postpartum obesity.** Exercise decreases the likelihood of postpartum obesity. Although it is certainly possible to reshape your body after pregnancy, the best way to counteract postpartum weight gain is to stay in shape during pregnancy. By dedicating yourself to a regimented workout schedule, you can recapture your original shape shortly after childbirth. Training allows you to preserve muscle mass throughout the term, keeping your resting metabolic rate elevated. Because activity levels tend to decrease during this period, sustaining your metabolism is extremely important as it helps to hinder excessive weight gain and make weight loss easier after delivery.

• **Physical and mental well-being.** Exercise improves physical and mental well-being during pregnancy. Pregnant women who remain active are less likely to lose their motivation and self-confidence. Training increases your energy levels, reduces fatigue, and promotes a better sense of well-being. This in turn boosts self-esteem so that you can fully appreciate this special period.

- **Reduced lower-back pain.** Exercise reduces the incidence of lower-back pain during pregnancy. Lower-back problems are one of the most common ailments experienced during pregnancy. Because a woman carries an extra 20 pounds or more in her abdominal region, a structural imbalance is created that places a great deal of stress on the lumbar region. If the muscles in this area are weak, stress is heightened, increasing the probability of developing lower-back pain. Exercise strengthens the associated musculature, improving posture and preventing potential problems. By maintaining muscular health, you can prevent many related anomalies, thus preserving your physical well-being.

- **Easier labor.** Exercise can foster an easier labor. One of a woman's worst fears during pregnancy is the thought of enduring a grueling, prolonged labor. Research suggests that continued exercise, particularly throughout late pregnancy, may have a positive effect on the course of labor. The increased strength and level of fitness acquired through a regimented exercise program improves placental growth and function, regulating contractions and facilitating a smooth delivery. Overall, the entire childbirth process is greatly enhanced, diminishing the pain and discomfort associated with labor.

Initial Safety Precautions

Before beginning a routine, you should first consult with your physician to rule out any possible contraindications for exercise. Conditions such as hypertension, bleeding, cardiac arrhythmia, and other health problems are potentially injurious. Even conditions that seem innocuous under normal circumstances can become acutely problematic during the physical changes of pregnancy. Therefore, medical clearance is a necessary prerequisite before undertaking a training regimen, and you should obtain regular follow-ups to monitor changes in your health. In this case, an ounce of prevention really is worth a pound of cure.

Of course, common sense should prevail here. If you were sedentary before conception, you will need to work into a program at a much slower pace than a woman who is physically fit. If you've never trained before, now is not the time to get bold.

To derive proper benefits, you must understand the unique nuances of working out during pregnancy. When you are pregnant, your response to physical activity changes substantially. You simply cannot train at high-energy levels and must restrict some of your actions and motions for the sake of your baby's health. Your fitness goal during this period is not to optimize your physique but rather to maintain a high level of fitness consistent with maximum safety. By following certain basic guidelines and remaining diligent in the pursuit of your goals, you can reap the rewards of staying fit during and after the pregnancy—without risking injury to yourself or your fetus.

Regardless of your level of fitness, a pregnancy workout will take longer than usual. You must do everything at a deliberate, leisurely pace. To prepare your body adequately, spend extra time in the warm-up. Proceed through your routine with caution, taking as much time as necessary to keep your heart rate within acceptable levels.

Creating a Pregnancy Routine

If no unusual circumstances exist, you are ready to begin training. The structure of your workout will be largely the same as in the body-conditioning phase of this system, with adjustments for the physical constraints of pregnancy. You employ a combination of stretching, weight training, and cardiovascular exercise, with set and rep schemes similar to those outlined earlier for the body-conditioning phase (see chapter 3). You should plan to exercise at regular intervals using the same three-day-per-week training schedule advocated earlier this book (for example, Monday, Wednesday, and Friday). Adequate rest is particularly important at this time, and you must listen to your body. Accordingly, if you feel at all fatigued, allow an additional day or two of recuperation.

A consideration vital to prenatal health is maintaining stable body temperature while training. Some research suggests that pregnancy increases your internal temperature, predisposing your body to overheating (a condition called hyperthermia). Exercising in a hot, humid place makes it difficult for your body to cool itself, substantially increasing the risk of heat-related illness. Thus, you must make sure that your training facility is well ventilated and air conditioned, allowing your body to remain cool throughout the workout. In addition, dress appropriately when you work out: supportive shoes to maintain balance, a maternity bra with lots of support, and temperature-appropriate clothes (tights and layers in cold temperatures, cotton T-shirts and shorts in warm temperatures) are requisite. Monitor your body temperature throughout your workout. If you notice any sharp variances, stop training immediately.

It is also important to remain well hydrated throughout your workout. Severe dehydration can lead to heat exhaustion or even heat stroke with potentially disastrous consequences. Therefore, you should consume up to a pint of liquid before exercise and a minimum of one cup for every 20 minutes of training. This ensures adequate fluid replacement to replenish water lost through perspiration. A final warning: don't use thirst as a measure of hydration. By the time you're thirsty, your body is already becoming dehydrated!

As always, begin your workout with a warm-up. This is especially important during pregnancy. Hormonal changes associated with pregnancy cause a softening of your connective tissue. This in turn relaxes your ligaments, making them unstable and susceptible to injury. A proper warm-up helps circulate blood throughout your body, alleviating stress in the joints and thereby decreasing the risk of impairment. Use a program similar to the one in chapter 2, taking extra time to ensure that your body is thoroughly warm. To reduce risk further, never stretch to the point of maximum resistance. Instead, perform stretches in a relaxed manner and stay within a comfortable zone. Of course, you should avoid any ballistic, bouncing movements, which are especially hazardous at this time.

■ Staying hydrated will help you through your workout and it's good for the baby!

213

Next, you should move on to a regimented weight-training routine. It is unfortunate that many women abandon weight-bearing exercise at the onset of pregnancy. There is a mistaken belief that weight training is "too dangerous" during pregnancy, with limited benefits because of physical restrictions. But as long as you follow established protocols, weight training is perfectly safe. Moreover, it is the only modality that allows you to preserve lean muscle tissue, preventing your metabolism from slowing to a crawl. If you want to stay in shape during pregnancy, you need to lift weights!

As in the body-conditioning phase, use a total-body workout as the basis of your routine. This directs blood flow to all areas of the body, ensuring adequate circulation to the fetus throughout your workout. Moreover, each muscle group continually receives direct stimulus, helping to maintain overall fitness levels.

You must, however, substantially modify your training regimen to accommodate the demands of pregnancy. There are many contraindications to exercise, and anything that might jeopardize the pregnancy is explicitly taboo.

Pregnancy Training Protocol

In order to get the most out of the pregnancy training component of this system, adhere to the following protocol:

- **Exercises.** Use only one exercise per muscle group, training your entire body during each workout. It is still beneficial to vary your exercises, making sure to avoid the contraindicated movements covered later in this chapter. Remember, though, that your focus is on maintaining a high level of fitness, not on bodysculpting. Hence, keep your workout simple and concentrate on basic movements. Discard from your routine any exercise that you find uncomfortable to perform, substituting movements more appropriate to your present status.

- **Sets.** When you are pregnant, the number of sets that you perform will vary based on your energy reserves. At the onset of pregnancy, you should strive to perform three sets of each exercise, an ideal scheme for virtually all fitness goals. This sufficiently stimulates your muscle fibers without overtraining your body. As your pregnancy progresses, adjust the volume of exercise according to your stamina. If you feel overtired toward the end of your workout, lighten the workload by paring down to two, or even one, set per exercise.

- **Rest.** The pace of a pregnancy routine is decidedly slower than normal, with rest intervals of one minute or more between sets. Unlike high-energy workouts, weight training during pregnancy should not be an aerobic endeavor. Because pregnancy results in an increase in weight and reduced oxygen efficiency, your body requires longer rest intervals to maintain strength and energy reserves. As a rule, allow your heart rate to return to near resting levels before beginning a new set. But avoid remaining stationary between sets; this can decrease your cardiac output and bring about cardiovascular complications. By simply walking around slowly after you finish a set, you maintain healthy circulation and avert potential problems.

- **Repetitions.** During pregnancy, it is especially important to use a high-repetition scheme. The target range should never be lower than 15 reps per set. Obviously, you are not training for strength or power, and high reps are beneficial for protecting your joints and connective tissue from inflammation. Repetitions should be smooth and controlled, with particular emphasis on maintaining form. A variety of complications can arise should you swing or jerk up a weight while lifting. Use special care to work through a functional range of motion. Moreover, be sure to regulate your breathing on each rep, keeping it slow and rhythmic. Never hold your breath during a lift, which increases intra-abdominal pressure and heightens your risk of becoming dizzy or fainting.

• **Intensity.** You should perform all sets with a weight that is somewhat challenging. Never should you struggle to complete a set, as training too intensely during pregnancy can have disastrous ramifications. Use extreme caution in this regard. Your aim is to induce mild muscular stimulation, not strain your resources. If a set becomes difficult, don't hesitate to stop short of completing it. Although you may tend to become caught up in the moment, you must use restraint when lifting, making sure not to push too hard. Training during pregnancy is not a high-energy endeavor!

Pregnancy Training Protocol

Number of exercises:	1 per muscle group
Number of sets:	1–3 per exercise
Rest between sets:	1 minute or more
Repetitions per set:	15–20
Intensity:	Somewhat challenging

The pregnancy training protocol summarizes the protocol for pregnancy training. I cannot overemphasize the importance of taking this protocol seriously. Pregnancy is a complex state with so many variables that there is little margin for error. On the other hand, it can be detrimental to be overcautious in your training philosophy. This can lead to a tentative approach that may result in injury. The best way to train is to understand all the variables, stay relaxed, and train within your limitations.

Contraindications to Exercise During Pregnancy

Many exercises are contraindicated during pregnancy. Because of the physiological and hormonal changes, certain movements are potentially harmful not only to you but also to your fetus. To avoid possible problems, you should understand the reasons for these contraindications. This allows you to determine whether an exercise is safe based on how it is executed.

1. Avoid exercises that incorporate bending from the waist or hips after the first trimester. Because of the uneven weight distribution in pregnancy, bending can be uncomfortable. During exercise, movements that require bending can lead to a variety of complications, including dizziness and heartburn. Moreover, they tend to place undue stress on the lumbar region, possibly causing injury to the lower back. These can be precursors to other, more serious problems. Thus, you should not perform exercises such as the stiff-legged dead lift and bent row after the first three months of pregnancy. As a substitute, you can use modified positions, such as elbows and knees or all fours to target the gluteal and hamstring area. If necessary, you can facilitate these movements with towels or pillows to maintain proper body alignment.

2. Abandon all overhead lifting exercises after the first trimester. Although exercise can strengthen the muscles of the lower back, you must pay special heed to this area during pregnancy. As previously noted, lower-back pain is one of the most common ailments experienced by pregnant women. Because of postural changes, overhead exercises tend to increase pressure on the lower back, making it vulnerable to injury. As the pregnancy progresses, structural imbalances are

magnified. Thus, you should not use exercises such as the military press and incline press.

3.   Abandon exercises performed in the supine position after the first trimester. Because of the redistribution of circulatory flow, pregnant women are prone to low blood pressure (hypotension). Exercises performed in the supine position can exacerbate this condition, causing a woman to become light-headed and dizzy. Furthermore, these exercises allow the fetus to press on the vena cava, decreasing blood flow to the fetus. When circulation is obstructed, oxygen supply to the fetus is reduced, which can cause dire complications. Thus, omit exercises such as the bench press, crunch, lying triceps extension, and so forth after the third month.

Although these restrictions limit your training alternatives, you still have many exercises from which to choose. Table 16.1 shows a sample weight-training routine that incorporates the principles just discussed and demonstrates the potential for adding variety and interest to your program. If you are creative, you'll find a myriad of possibilities at your disposal.

Cardio and Flexibility Training During Pregnancy

You should cap off your workout with a period of cardiovascular activity. Here, too, safety is a critical issue, and you must observe several restrictions. Limit your aerobic activity to 20 minutes or so. Your heart rate should not exceed approximately 70 percent of your age-related maximum. A good way to monitor your intensity is to use a technique called the talk test. The talk test is based on your ability to speak in complete sentences without gasping for breath. If you are unable to carry on a conversation, the work rate is too hard, and you should reduce your level of effort. Although the talk test errs on the side of caution, it keeps you within a safe training range and helps to ensure an acceptable training intensity.

I do not recommend aerobics classes, especially high-impact and step aerobics, during pregnancy. In chapter 15, I discussed the drawbacks of these classes, which are of even greater concern during this period. Because of the joint instability associated with pregnancy, you are particularly vulnerable to stressful activities.

TABLE 16.1   SAMPLE THREE-DAY PREGNANCY WEIGHT-TRAINING PROGRAM

MUSCLE GROUP	DAY 1	DAY 2	DAY 3
Chest	Seated row	Straight-arm pull-down	Dumbbell row
Back	Lateral raise	Upright row	Front raise
Shoulders	Pec deck	Cable crossover	Modified push-up
Biceps	Seated dumbbell curl	EZ curl	Cable curl
Triceps	Press-down	Kickback	Triceps dip
Quadriceps	Leg extension	Lunge	Seated leg press
Hamstrings and glutes	Standing leg curl	Abductor pull	Floor kick
Calves	Seated calf raise	Standing calf raise	Toe press
Abdominals	Rope crunch	Bench leg raise	Side twist

The bouncing movements, jumping motions, and rapid directional changes inherent to aerobics classes exert heavy stress on the body, often causing strains, sprains, or even fractures of the extremities. Moreover, because postural changes of pregnancy distort your equilibrium, you may find it difficult to maintain balance while performing movements in these classes. This can lead to slips or falls—a dangerous prospect at this time.

For the cardiovascular component of your workout, it is best to adhere to a routine that uses individual activities. Exercises such as the treadmill, stationary bike, and stair climber are fine choices. These modalities allow you to remain in control during exercise and are flexible enough that you can adapt them to your abilities. They ensure a high degree of safety and produce optimal results.

After cardio, it is best to finish the workout with gentle stretching movements, following the principles described in chapter 2. This gradually stabilizes your body temperature and helps flush lactic acid from your working muscles. Stretch for as long as you desire, making sure you have completely cooled down before leaving the gym.

Other Pregnancy-Related Issues

If no complications arise during your pregnancy, you can continue with this program nearly until term. As long as you have the energy and motivation, there is no risk in training right up to delivery. Although you may want to reduce the frequency or length of your sessions, your routine can continue as described without ill effect. The numerous benefits of exercise make it advantageous to continue with your program as long as you can.

After childbirth, you should normally be able to return to exercise within three to four weeks. Again, check with your physician before resuming your training regimen. When you return, you should begin as if you were starting from scratch. Because many of the physiological and morphological changes of pregnancy persist for up to six weeks after delivery, you should resume training gradually. Consider yourself a beginner again, and follow the protocol outlined in the body-conditioning routine (see chapter 3). With diligence, you will quickly achieve your previous level of fitness.

That's it: a comprehensive routine that is safe and effective. Your entire pregnancy workout will last about an hour to an hour and a half and should leave you feeling healthy and invigorated. By following the principles and dedicating yourself to a regimented workout schedule, you can maintain your shape throughout pregnancy and ultimately look as good as or better than you did before conception!

Maintaining Your Physique

17

Your journey to physique heaven is almost complete. After training in the advanced phase of this system, the world of bodysculpting is now your oyster. You are the master of your physique, in complete control of your physical destiny—what a powerful feeling! You are now at a crossroads in your training endeavors and must decide which route you want to take.

Before determining a course of action, you must evaluate your options and match them with your training goals. Even at advanced levels, training is a dynamic process that demands constant attention to detail. To make an intelligent decision when going forward, you must know where you are and in what direction you want to go. Accordingly, these are some of the issues to contemplate: Are you satisfied with your present condition? Do you want to be in your best shape year-round? Are you prepared to continue training at maximum intensity? How you answer these questions will dictate your training philosophy from here on out.

Detraining

If you want to hold onto your hard-earned gains, there is no getting around the fact that you need to keep up your fitness regimen. Exercise is a lifetime commitment that requires consistent participation to sustain a high degree of muscle tone. Although you may theorize that it will no longer be necessary to train once you attain your ideal physique, nothing could be further from the truth. In fact, you'll have to train as hard as you did before, if not harder, if you intend to make continued aesthetic improvements to your body.

After working so diligently to perfect your physique, it would be a shame to see it deteriorate. But that's exactly what will happen if you stop working out. During such a period, called detraining, your muscles gradually start to atrophy (decrease in size), losing their hardness and density. Along with this loss of muscle tissue, your metabolism begins to slow down, causing a corresponding increase in body-fat storage. Over time, your physique returns to pretraining levels. Alas, you will eventually look as if you had never even worked out.

Fortunately, you can take heart in the fact that detraining does not take place overnight. Your body craves stability and tries to establish a comfort zone at a given set point (a phenomenon called homeostasis). Once your body establishes this set point, it attempts to maintain homeostasis by defending itself against any shift away from this state. Thus, if you have kept yourself in peak condition for a substantial time, your body will strive to stay in shape, using all its resources to avoid a loss of muscle tissue.

Although individual factors determine the actual rate of detraining, you'll experience virtually no change in body composition from a brief layoff. On average, muscular atrophy is negligible for up to two weeks of inactivity. In fact, a short period of inactivity can be beneficial to your body, providing increased stamina for future workouts (if you have been training consistently for a substantial time).

After two weeks, the effects of detraining will begin to become apparent. Still, you should notice only a modest decline in body composition after a month without exercising. And even after a six-month hiatus, you can maintain as much as 50 percent of your gains, giving your body at least a semblance of firmness.

Moreover, it is significantly easier to regain your previous shape after a layoff. Because of a phenomenon known as muscle memory, your body is sensitized to recover lost muscle tissue when you return to training. Although there is no definitive scientific explanation for this curiosity, it is a fact that your body responds more rapidly to exercise the second time around. On average, you can expect to shape your ideal physique in roughly half the time it took in the past.

Although you should avoid detraining at all costs, it sometimes becomes inevitable. If you must undergo a prolonged period of inactivity for any reason (injury, family crisis, or other circumstance), you will need to reacclimate your muscles to the training process. Your initial reaction might be to jump back into your routine and make up for lost time, but you must resist this imprudent temptation. Once detraining has occurred, your body has a reduced capacity for exertion. Although your mind might be willing to train all out, your body isn't able to handle such a high level of intensity. Attempting to do the workout you were once accustomed to would cause severe trauma to your entire neuromuscular system, potentially leading to serious injury.

Accordingly, you should take a cautious approach upon your return. Because the extent of detraining is directly correlated to the duration of inactivity, you should progress at a pace consistent with the length of time you have been sedentary. This ensures that you don't overtax your neuromuscular system, and it helps to prevent a debilitating injury that could derail your comeback efforts.

©Image State

■ Beware of detraining for long periods of time—strive to stay at peak condition.

MUSCLE AND FAT

There is a prevailing misconception that if you stop lifting weights, the muscle-building process reverses and all the muscle that you've acquired just turns into fat. This belief is often an argument against resistance training. After all, why go to all the trouble of building your muscles if they're just going to morph into adipose tissue once training is discontinued?

The truth is, however, that muscle and fat are two separate and distinct tissues that have completely different molecular structures. Muscle is a protein-based tissue composed of filaments called actin and myosin. These filaments are derived from various amino acids and carry out a plethora of metabolic functions. Body fat, on the other hand, is stored triglycerides. Triglycerides are made up of a carbohydrate portion (glycerol) and three fatty acids. Once formed, triglycerides are packaged into cells called adipocytes (fat cells) and are used primarily as a long-term energy source. In its stored form, fat is biologically inert with little purpose other than to provide fuel and insulation. Hence, the possibility of muscle turning into fat (or vice versa) is akin to an apple becoming an orange: There's simply no mechanism for it to happen.

Furthermore, it's a common mistake to maintain the same caloric intake during a layoff from training as during training. Because muscle raises your resting metabolic rate and allows the body to burn more calories, you can consume more food when you are participating in a fitness program. But when you stop training, it is essential to reassess your eating habits and take in fewer calories to account for the slowdown in metabolism. If you don't cut back on your caloric intake, you'll experience weight gain and see the *illusion* of your muscle turning into fat.

In general, you need make only minor modifications to your routine if your layoff was less than three months in duration. In your first workout, reduce exercise intensity so that you aren't struggling to complete your final few reps. Rest slightly longer than normal, taking up to a minute between sets. It is best to avoid using any supersets or giant sets, concentrating solely on regaining your strength and endurance. Over the next several workouts, you can begin to increase intensity and reduce rest intervals, gradually working back to previous levels. Within a month, you can resume training in a high-energy format and should be close to being your best.

On the other hand, if your layoff extended more than three months, it is prudent to start from the beginning. You'll need to reestablish your motor skills and rebuild a foundation of muscle. To accomplish this objective, you should use the body-conditioning phase of this system (see chapter 3), training your entire body at each workout.

During your first few weeks, make sure to take things in a slow, deliberate fashion. Your focus should be on regenerating the neuromuscular pathways necessary for optimal performance. It will take some time to get back into a training groove, and you must be patient in your efforts. Once you have accomplished these objectives, you should continue through the system in a stepwise fashion. With diligence, you will be able to make rapid progress, returning to your prior condition within a few months.

Creating a Maintenance Routine

Assuming that you are willing and able to keep up your fitness regimen (and have not experienced a long layoff), you now must decide whether you want to actualize your full potential or simply maintain your present body composition. If you are content with your level of development or no longer wish to train with all-out intensity, then maintenance is a viable option.

But don't expect the maintenance routine to be a walk in the park. You cannot simply go through the motions and magically expect to retain your proportions. On the contrary, if you slack off for a prolonged period, you'll experience a gradual breakdown of muscle tissue. Although this decline won't be as severe as if you discontinued training altogether (any stimulus is better than none), a prolonged period of reduced effort will certainly degrade the quality of your physique. Unless you'll be satisfied with losing some of your hard-earned gains, you must be willing to exert maximal effort at least occasionally.

To maintain your physique at optimal levels, you'll be best served by using a technique called periodization. Simply stated, periodization (sometimes referred to as cycling) is a structured way to vary your workouts at regular time intervals. You do this by altering one or more training variables in a progressive format to attain a variety of training goals.

Bodybuilders often use a periodized program to peak for a competition, structuring their routines into heavy, medium, and light cycles. For instance, a periodized bodybuilding routine normally begins with a heavy cycle. During this phase, the bodybuilder trains for strength; the goal is to bulk up and get as strong as possible. Next, the bodybuilder uses a medium cycle, attempting to maximize muscular hypertrophy and bring each muscle into aesthetic proportion. Finally, the competitor employs a light cycle, attempting to bring out maximum muscular detail and strip away all excess body fat. Properly executed, this routine molds strength, size, and definition into perfect symmetry, creating a classic bodybuilding physique.

Although periodization is most commonly associated with sports training and bodybuilding, it can be modified to work beautifully as a maintenance strategy. Because your body strives to preserve homeostasis, you can retain a high degree of muscle tone with only sporadic bouts of all-out training. By employing alternating cycles of maximal and submaximal effort, you can exert enough neuromuscular stimulus to retain your shape but still enjoy periods of carefree training.

In the maintenance program, you continue to use the targeted bodysculpting phase of this system while structuring your routine into three distinct cycles: low intensity, medium intensity, and high intensity. You perform each cycle for a month, repeating the procedure at the end of the third month. You keep all other training variables constant, including high reps and brief rest intervals. This ensures that you preserve your aerobic conditioning and metabolic state, minimizing gains in body fat.

Maintenance Protocol

In order to get the most out of the maintenance component of this system, adhere to the following protocol:

• **Month 1 (low-intensity cycle):** During this cycle, you should train at submaximal intensity, using weights that are challenging but not arduous. The objective of this phase is to preserve a basic level of conditioning and prevent a tangible loss of muscle tone. You should focus on keeping a quick pace in your routine, moving freely from one movement to the next. There is no need to struggle at this point, because muscular failure is not the goal. Although this phase will produce a mild aerobic effect, it won't tax your resources, nor will it cause significant muscular fatigue. If you truly loathe the muscular pain associated with high-energy training, you should enjoy this phase of your workout!

- **Month 2 (moderate-intensity cycle):** During this cycle, you up the intensity a notch. The objective here is to bridge back to high-energy levels, preparing your body for all-out training. Your workouts will now require more physical exertion, and you should feel reasonably fatigued by the end of your session. Although you won't be training to failure, the last few reps of a set should be somewhat of a struggle to complete. Still, this phase won't produce the severe muscular discomfort associated with high-energy training.

- **Month 3 (high-intensity cycle):** During this cycle, you should train with all-out intensity, taking your sets to momentary muscular failure. The objective here is to shock your system, maximally stimulating all your muscle fibers. You will now be training in a true high-energy format, with the intention of pushing yourself to the limit. This is the most important phase of the maintenance cycle because it fully taxes your resources and forces your body to maintain homeostasis at elite levels. Remember: unless you go all out in your efforts, you won't stress your body enough to keep your hard-earned gains.

Psychological Aspects of Maintenance

Let me warn you that you must deal with some psychological ramifications of this maintenance program. During the low-intensity cycles, it is quite common to feel as though you are out of shape. "I feel soft and flabby" is a frequent lament during these periods. This is just a subjective perception, however. As previously stated, once you have developed a high degree of muscular conditioning, detraining does not occur this rapidly. Although a slight degradation in your body composition is inevitable when you decrease training intensity, you quickly regenerate any loss of muscle in your high-energy cycle.

Maintenance training, however, is not for everyone. Although many women are content when they attain a certain level of development, others are never satisfied no matter how far they progress. If you possess a drive that compels you to be your best, then you won't be content using a maintenance program. Rather, you'll need to train in a fashion conducive to the ongoing pursuit of physical perfection.

Unfortunately, the closer you come to your potential, the harder it will be to make tangible improvements in your physique. Remember that you achieve muscle development through your body's response to intense neuromuscular stress. This response is your body's defense mechanism against its next encounter with strong neuromuscular stimulus.

As you move along the path toward physique heaven, you will experience diminishing returns from your efforts. Your body begins to adapt to the intense stress of exercise and becomes less inclined to respond to a training stimulus. Moreover, because you are in much better physical condition, any enhancement in body composition will be more subtle.

Correspondingly, the closer you come to actualizing your potential, the less room you have for improvement. No one, however, can achieve physical perfection. Regardless of your level of development, there will forever be areas of your physique that can be improved. You ultimately will become a physique connoisseur, seeking to tighten, shape, or tone certain body parts. Fortunately, you'll always be able to make alterations to your physique, provided that you are willing to put in the effort.

To make tangible improvements, you must continually force your body to adapt to the stresses of exercise. The only way to accomplish this is by constantly keeping your body off guard, never allowing it to adjust to your training regimen. You'll need to use all of your training knowledge to manipulate your routine for optimal effect. For instance, you can employ different bodysculpting techniques, alter the split of your routine, use different exercise equipment—whatever you have to do to confuse your body and compel it to respond.

Mental focus is especially important at this level. Your mind can push your body to do things you may have never imagined, allowing you to soar to incredible heights. Harnessing all your mental capacity is crucial to working past the pain threshold, a limiting factor in aesthetic development. Mental strength allows you to elevate your training intensity repeatedly, taxing your body in the manner necessary to make ongoing improvements.

One of the biggest mistakes you can make at advanced levels is becoming caught up in a train-at-all-costs mentality. After years of working out, training often turns into a ritual. It can become like a drug, taking over your mind, body, and spirit. Many psychological motivations perpetuate this obsession. Perhaps you crave the special feeling of having a great body and feel out of shape after missing a workout. Perhaps you have built a social network and don't want to miss seeing your friends. Or perhaps you use your workout as a means of escaping the problems of everyday life and feel stressed out when you don't train. These and other factors can exert a powerful influence that compels you to exercise.

In extreme cases, a training addiction can become so severe that it causes you to experience withdrawal symptoms when you miss as much as a single training session. This can result in a severe case of overtraining. Throughout this book, I have repeatedly warned about the deleterious effects that overtraining can have on your body. Not only will it prohibit you from making further gains, but it actually breaks down your muscle tissue, thereby diminishing the quality of your physique.

Although a three-day-per-week regimen is generally sufficient for adequate recuperation, you'll occasionally need additional recovery time. The demands of intense training combined with external factors (such as sleeping patterns, stress levels, or nutritional deficiencies) can sometimes overwhelm your body and weaken your immune function, making necessary an extra day or two of rest. This is especially true at advanced levels, where the ravages of sustained high-energy training begin to take a toll on your body. Therefore, you must always be in tune with your sense of being; if you feel weak or depleted and need an extra day off, take it! If you can't train at sufficient intensity, it is better to rest a day and come back stronger the next.

Avoid being blinded by emotion, ignoring your body's telltale signs. Although it is natural to feel that adding more sets or training more frequently will produce better gains, this most often is not the case. Don't lose sight of the fact that recuperation, not the act of training, is what produces gains in muscle tone. For optimal results, be dispassionate in your approach and train scientifically, not haphazardly.

Some Final Words

No discussion of bodysculpting would be complete without mentioning the importance of diet. Nutrition is a complex subject that is beyond the scope of this book. A brief summary cannot do justice to the intricacies of this topic.

Needless to say, without a sensible nutritional regimen, you will never maximize your genetic potential. Diet is at least as important as training in achieving your ideal physique—maybe more so. It is essential in regulating body-fat storage and aiding the growth and repair of muscle tissue. I encourage you to learn as much as you can about the subject and develop a consistent dietary regimen that works for you. You might want to check out my book, *Look Great Naked* (Prentice Hall), which has several chapters dedicated to proper diet and discusses at length how to optimally manipulate nutritional variables to get your body into its optimal shape.

I hope this book has inspired you to take control of your body and maximize your genetic potential. Whatever your bodysculpting goals may be, you now have the knowledge to be your best. Knowledge is power, giving you the ability to soar to extraordinary heights. By embracing a fitness lifestyle, you will be sound in mind and body. With patience and persistence, you, like thousands of other women, can change your life forever.

I'll see you in physique heaven!